Dry Basement Science

What to Have Done... *and Why*

LAWRENCE JANESKY

Dry Basement Science

What to Have Done... *and Why*

BY LAWRENCE JANESKY

Published by:

Basement Systems, Inc.
60 Silvermine Road, Seymour, CT 06483
800.640.1500 | 203.881.5090
www.BasementSystems.com

8th Edition

Copyright ©2017. All Rights Reserved.

THIS BOOK IS DEDICATED TO the hard-working men and women at Basement Systems dealerships worldwide, who every day solve the mystery of how to turn wet or damp basements into comfortable, dry, usable space for homeowners.

Table of Contents

This is not a do-it-yourself book because basement waterproofing is not a do-it-yourself job. It's hard work, and takes specialized knowledge, skill and equipment.

The purpose of this book is to give you enough knowledge to make an educated decision on what work needs to be done to your home, who should do it, and why.

Foreword

Dry Basement Science. Don't let the title fool you. It's not that complicated. In fact, you will see why I nearly called the book Dry Basements: When Science Meets Common Sense.

What qualifies me to write this book? I am the founder and president of Basement Systems, Inc., the world's largest basement waterproofing company. Since the beginning, Basement Systems has actively sought better ways of doing things. We are not the kind of company that has a single year of experience twenty times; rather we are a learning organization, hell-bent on seeking the best way.

Basement Systems has developed a close network of like-minded basement waterproofing contractors who are dealers of our products (one of them probably gave you this book). We have more than 300 dealers in seven countries, some with more experience than me, who install the best basement waterproofing products and systems ever developed. We are not saying these products are the best because they are ours, but rather they are ours because they are the best. Without our more-than-significant efforts toward creating better ways of fixing wet basements, most of these products would not exist, as we invented and developed them.

Because we work with so many basement waterproofing specialists every day, and fix thousands of wet basements ourselves (since 1987 our Connecticut office alone has fixed over 32,000), we bring you the collective wisdom of thousands of experts and hundreds of thousands of jobs completed. It's all we do and we love it. That's what makes me an authority.

Basement waterproofing as a business has been around since the 1930s. Not a lot of new thinking had been applied until 1990 or so. Almost every other home improvement sector or appliance that you use has been modernized, changed and improved. Now it's time for basement waterproofing to come of age.

Your basement is useful space, easy to heat and cool, and easy to finish. A homebuyer will expect your basement to be dry. Since you can spend a lot of money and not get the result you wanted, this is an important subject.

If it's worth owning a home with a wet basement at all, it is certainly worth fixing...

Your local Basement Systems dealer may have given you this book. Otherwise, find your local Basement Systems dealer by calling the international headquarters at 800.640.1500 or visiting www.BasementSystems.com.

1 MAIN FACILITY

2 SUPPLY WAREHOUSE AND SOFTWARE PROGRAMMING

3 NEW LOCAL SERVICES FACILITY

4 DR. ENERGY SAVER INTERNATIONAL TRAINING CENTER

5 SPRAY FOAM, STRUCTURAL REPAIR, BASEMENT FINISHING

6 FLEET MAINTENANCE

7 SANIDRY AIR SYSTEM CENTER

8 RESEARCH AND DEVELOPMENT

9 DEALER SUPPLY WAREHOUSE AND TRAINING CENTER

What do you want?

Take the Quiz

FINISH THE NEXT TWO THOUGHTS BY CHOOSING A, B, OR C.

I want –

A) Part of my basement dry
You probably already have this, you can stop reading now.

B) Most of my basement dry
Then only treat part of your basement.

C) My WHOLE basement dry!
Then treat your WHOLE basement.

I want a dry basement –

A) When it doesn't rain.
You probably already have this, you can stop reading now.

B) Most of the time.
You probably have a dry basement most of the time like most wet basement sufferers. You can make it worse by spending SOME money on it, fix it halfway, and you will still have a dry basement only most of the time. (Arghhhh!)

C) ALL the time!
Then have it fixed right. Don't cheap out.

So the premise of this book is that you want your whole basement dry all the time. Read on...

Basement Terms of the Trade

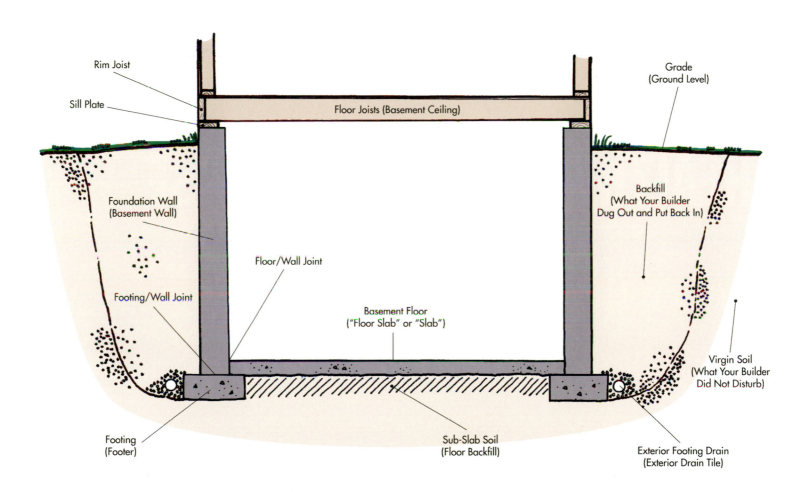

Rim Joist

Sill Plate

Floor Joists (Basement Ceiling)

Grade (Ground Level)

Foundation Wall (Basement Wall)

Backfill (What Your Builder Dug Out and Put Back In)

Floor/Wall Joint

Footing/Wall Joint

Basement Floor ("Floor Slab" or "Slab")

Virgin Soil (What Your Builder Did Not Disturb)

Footing (Footer)

Sub-Slab Soil (Floor Backfill)

Exterior Footing Drain (Exterior Drain Tile)

CHAPTER ONE

HEALTHY, WEALTHY AND WISE

How a Dry Basement Adds Value to Your Home

Your basement is not just a concrete-lined hole in the ground. It is valuable space. If it's wet, it can cost you big-time, upstairs and down, and its damp, moldy air can harm your family's health. If your basement is dry, on the other hand, it can be whatever you want it to be, and your house will fetch a higher price.

Your wet basement is worth fixing, and it's worth fixing right.

"GROUNDWATER LEAKS ARE NEVER COVERED"

Mr. and Mrs. Wetmore

had a home with a wet basement. For many years they chose to add optimism to the problem, believing it would go away due to various factors that the gods would put in their favor. Several times each year the air was filled with the sound of their wet vac, and grumbles of another "freak" situation. Years later, when trying to sell their home, the Wetmores found that potential buyers who liked their home would walk away once they got to the basement or the inspection stage, because they did not want to inherit a problem they viewed as unsolvable. Hence, the Wetmores couldn't sell their house.

Mr. Gill

wanted some space to call his own. The kids were getting older and taking up lots of space and making lots of noise upstairs. So he hired Billy Doright, carpenter extraordinaire, to finish the basement. "Does the basement ever leak?" Billy asked. "Not really," said Mr. Gill. So Billy hammered and drywalled and painted for weeks, finishing just in time for the Carpet World guys' installation date. Mr. Gill was so proud. One crisp morning Mr. Gill decided to run down to the basement to gaze at his new sanctuary for inspiration before going to work. He never made it to work. Instead he spent the day on the phone with his insurance company, only to find that his newly finished, and even more newly ruined finished basement was not covered. "Groundwater leaks are never covered." The words echoed in his head for weeks.

Mr. and Mrs. Rainwater's

basement flooded once. They cleaned the gutters just like their cousin told them to. After all, he was a builder and he knew about these things. They didn't see any more water in their basement for a good six months. They soon forgot about the incident and put all their stuff on the basement floor. There was holiday stuff, tax records, an LP collection, personal effects – even Mrs. Rainwater's preserved wedding dress, in a cardboard box like most of the other items. One otherwise peaceful evening, the sky opened up, as it does once every year or two, and two months' worth of rain fell in two days. All the belongings stored in the Rainwaters' basement were lost in the ensuing flood.

Mr. and Mrs. Spore moved their three small children into a new-to-them home. They knew the basement "had some issues," but felt they could deal with that later. After some time, two of the children began having asthma-like symptoms. When they went to school, they were better. When they came home, they puffed up again, and stuff leaked from their faces. What was in the home that was causing it? After hiring an indoor air quality consultant, they found the cause: mold in the basement from the slight but chronic seepage. "We can get rid of the mold," the expert said. "Will it grow back?" asked Mrs. Spore. "If the basement still leaks it could grow back," the expert said. And so it did. Mrs. Spore dealt with the mold issue by having her pediatrician prescribe these great allergy drugs, which she fed to her children to keep the symptoms at bay.

Mrs. Soker lived with her basement water problem for all of her forty years in the home at 14 Elm Street. She just couldn't see spending more than a few hundred dollars to fix it, and all the "experts" wanted much more than that. "Don't do it, Ma," her concerned son advised by phone from Seattle. "They're just trying to take advantage of you, being a widow and all." So she lived with it. Years later, when her surviving son, Mr. Soker, flew in to handle the executor's duties, he was told by the real estate agent that the only way the home could be sold was to fix the basement properly. So he did, using funds from the estate. Poor Mrs. Soker. For 40 years she had to put up with a wet basement.

Mrs. Soker's neighbor, **Mrs. Wright**, took a different road. She had her basement properly fixed long ago, and she was spared the financial and emotional cost that became the fate of her dear neighbor. "If I had known about this before, I'd have fixed it 15 years ago," was her only regret.

These stories of senseless loss are repeated every day.
Will you have a similar story?

You Breathe Basement Air – Like It or Not

As warm air rises in a home it leaks out of the upper levels. New air must enter to replace the air that escaped. In fact, in an average home about half of the air escapes each hour out of the upper levels. This creates a suction at the lower levels to draw in replacement air. In older, leaky homes the air exchange rate can be so high that a full air exchange takes place in a single hour.

What this "stack effect" does is create an airflow in your home from bottom to top. Air from the basement is drawn upward into the first floor, and then to the second floor. Of course it dilutes with other air in your home, but building scientists say that up to 50% of the air you breathe on the first floor is air that came from the basement. If you have hot air heating with ductwork, the air mixes even more thoroughly throughout the house.

Therefore, whatever is in your basement air is in your house and affecting you, whether you spend much time in the basement or not. If there's high humidity downstairs, there is higher humidity upstairs than there would be otherwise. If there is mold in the basement, there are mold spores upstairs. If there are damp odors downstairs — you get the idea.

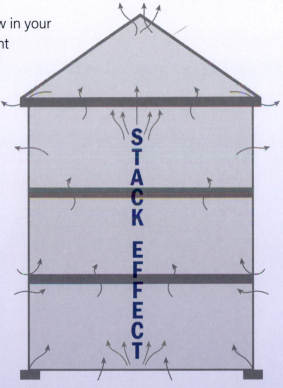

STACK EFFECT

Air leaking out at the top causes air to leak in at the bottom.

Prove It!
DO THIS TEST.

In the winter, go into your basement and open a window a bit. Feel the cold air blasting in at you? Close the window.

Now go upstairs – to the second floor if you have one. Crack open a window an inch or so. You don't feel any cold air blasting in? **Why not?** Because warm air is blasting **out**.

With low air pressure on the lower levels, your house sucks on the ground, then blows air out of the upper levels due to a higher air pressure.

To Your Health

(and if not yours, then theirs)

You can't find a doctor who says mold in a home is good. You can't find a doctor who says mold in your home is not bad. It's bad. It's all bad.

Besides irritating people with asthma and mold allergies, studies show that prolonged exposure to mold can actually cause asthma.

Mold = Bad

"Just Add Water"
Negative Effects of a Damp Basement

Since air flows into the upper levels of your home from the basement, it brings the humidity from the basement with it. The effects on your home can include:

- **Dust mites** (the number one indoor allergen)
- **Sticking** (swollen) doors and windows
- **Smelly damp carpets**
- **Buckling hardwood floors**
- **Condensation/rotting/mold in your attic** (as humid air escapes into your attic it can condense against the cold ceiling or roof)
- **Frost or condensation and mold** on the inside of windows in cool weather
- **Increased cooling bills** (damp air takes more energy to cool)
- **Increased heating bills** (damp air takes more energy to heat)
- **Mold upstairs**
- **Decreased life of roof sheathing and shingles**
- **Decreased life of the paint on the outside of your house**
- **Aggravated asthma and allergies**

The damage in the basement itself is obvious. The above list represents many of the effects upstairs that you may not associate with your wet or damp basement.

Dust Mites
#1 INDOOR ALLERGEN

Dust Mites are parasites that live in your carpeting, bedding and furniture. They are tiny – you can't see them. Their droppings are even smaller, and float in the air. These droppings are the number one thing people with asthma and allergies react to indoors.

What you need to know about dust mites is that they don't drink water, but instead absorb water out of the air. When the relative humidity is more than 50%, dust mites thrive. When the relative humidity goes down below 50%, they dry up and die. (However, they leave their larvae behind to hatch when it gets damp again.) Of course, when they die, they stop pooping. So the best way to combat dust mites is to dry up your wet basement and then keep the relative humidity down below 50%.

See Chapter 8 for more on humidity control.

Your Basement
Extra Space for Living!

What can you do with your basement?

- Playroom
- Billiard Room
- Party Room
- Family Room/Den/TV Room
- Art Room
- Teen Bedroom
- Home Office
- Bedrooms

- In-Law Apartment
- Home Gym
- Potting Room
- Model Train Set
- Home Theater
- Library
- Wine Cellar
- Extra Bathroom

- Sauna
- Record Storage
- Sewing Room
- Basement Bar
- Computer Room
- Cedar Closet
- Arts/Crafts Room

10% is a lot of money!

Because buyers view your home with a wet basement as a fixer-upper, they will pay you 10% less than otherwise – that's if they buy it at all. Using this example, then

Value of Your Home	The cost of not fixing your wet basement in **property value** alone
$100,000	$10,000
$150,000	$15,000
$200,000	$20,000
$300,000	$30,000
$400,000	$40,000
$500,000	$50,000
$600,000	$60,000

You get the idea. And this does not take into account all the property damage and other aggravation that the leak causes you while you live there! **Moral of the Story: Fixing your wet basement is a lot cheaper than not fixing your wet basement.**

Basement Space is Cheaper than Addition Space

To get more space in your home you can put an addition on at around $120 to $220 a square foot, or finish the basement at $50 to $70 per square foot. Now there's a bargain! But you can't finish your basement if it's wet — not even a little bit wet, not even a little bit of the time!

Even Unfinished Space = Finished Space

So you're not going to finish your basement, you say? Well, your unfinished space is just as valuable as finished space. Why? Because all the stuff that you'd normally keep in your dry, unfinished basement is now upstairs taking up finished space! By drying the basement you can move all that stuff downstairs and reclaim your finished space!

Buyers Expect a Dry Basement

Who wants to buy a home with a wet basement? Nobody! It's difficult enough to find a buyer who wants your house, and heartbreaking when they walk away after looking at the basement.

These days in most states there are disclosure forms that ask the seller a whole range of questions about their knowledge of defects with the property. One of the questions asks if you ever had any water in the basement. In addition, most buyers hire home inspectors these days to inspect the property for defects. Home inspectors have a keen eye for water problems.

There is simply no hiding your wet basement when you sell your home. And if you do disclose your leaky basement, either nobody will buy, or they will make a low offer. In fact, buyers will discount the price of a home by 10% or more because of a wet basement.

FIX IT TO LIST IT

Spend More, Costs Less

Pick your situation below:

Expensive Area
ONE-STORY HOME

YOUR HOME	THE MATH
$350,000, 2,400 sq. ft. *Wet basement, only 1,200 sq. ft. usable*	$\dfrac{350,000}{1,200}=$ **$291** per usable sq. ft.
Add $8,000 to fix basement	
Total Cost $358,000 *2,400 sq. ft. usable*	$\dfrac{358,000}{2,400}=$ **$149** per usable sq. ft.

Expensive Area
TWO-STORY HOME

YOUR HOME	THE MATH
$450,000, 3,000 sq. ft. *Wet basement, only 2,000 sq. ft. usable*	$\dfrac{450,000}{2,000}=$ **$225** per usable sq. ft.
Add $8,000 to fix basement	
Total Cost $458,000 *3,000 sq. ft. usable*	$\dfrac{458,000}{3,000}=$ **$152** per usable sq. ft.

Less Expensive Area
ONE-STORY HOME

YOUR HOME	THE MATH
$120,000, 2,400 sq. ft. *Wet basement, only 1,200 sq. ft. usable*	$\dfrac{120,000}{1,200} =$ **$100** per usable sq. ft.
Add $8,000 to fix basement	
Total Cost $128,000 *2,400 sq. ft. usable*	$\dfrac{128,000}{2,400} =$ **$53** per usable sq. ft.

Less Expensive Area
TWO-STORY HOME

YOUR HOME	THE MATH
$210,000, 3,000 sq. ft. *Wet basement, only 2,000 sq. ft. usable*	$\dfrac{210,000}{2,000} =$ **$105** per usable sq. ft.
Add $8,000 to fix basement	
Total Cost $218,000 *3,000 sq. ft. usable*	$\dfrac{218,000}{3,000} =$ **$73** per usable sq. ft.

CHAPTER TWO

WHY BASEMENTS LEAK
Designed for Failure

When builders build homes, they have a lot of things to put into the house and pay for. Given the choice of spending money on beautiful things like great cabinets and bathroom fixtures or on hidden things that protect the house and make it last longer, the builder goes for the beauty. **Why? That's what people see and want.**

There are two things that a builder can do to keep a basement from leaking:

1. A coating on the basement walls
2. A proper drain around the bottom of the foundation — called a "footing drain"

Wall coatings can be inexpensive black tar coatings called "damp-proofing." Damp-proofing costs builders about 20 cents per square foot, or around $200 a home. It doesn't bridge wall cracks, doesn't stop water completely, and doesn't last forever. Until about 1985, nearly all new homes were damp-proofed.

Even today, 85% of homes still only get their foundation walls damp-proofed.

A big step up from damp-proofing is a waterproof coating. This will cost a builder from 60 cents to $1.25 per square foot, or $1000 or more per home. It often includes drainage board or protection board, such as foam, over them. Waterproofing will bridge most small wall cracks, and will last a lot longer than damp-proofing.

Footing drains are plastic pipes with holes or slots. These pipes are laid around the outside of the footing or at the bottom of the walls. The idea is that the water flows through the slots into the pipes and is directed away from your basement. A bed of crushed stone is installed around the drain and the soil around the outside of your home is pushed back over it.

There are many things that can go wrong with footing drains — especially since unskilled labor is often used to install them. Problems include:

- **The drains don't lead out anywhere** — fairly common
- **The place they lead to is blocked, clogged or crushed** — fairly common
- **The drains clog as the water washing into them brings silt and sediment (mud) with it** — extremely common
- **The drains have very little or no stone around them** (stone is expensive)
- **The drains are not connected as a continuous loop or are installed too high**
- Etc. etc.

Footing Drain Failure

Footing drain failure is the most common cause of wet basements. When this happens, the soil around the outside of the foundation can't drain and becomes saturated. The weight of the water in the soil creates hydrostatic pressure and pushes the water into the basement through:

- **The joint between the footing and the wall** — most common
- **Wall cracks and pipe penetrations** — very common
- **Porous block walls** — very common if you have block walls.
- **Under the footing** — pretty rare

Big ifs. Exterior footing drains work if installed properly and if they don't clog.

Stone Under the Floor is Helpful

By installing stone aggregate under the floor instead of just dirt, the builder can help water that does get under the floor drain to a sump location. There are also inexpensive drainage flashings, such as CactusBoard floor edging, that builders can install around the perimeter of the floor. The problem is that stone can cost $400 to $600 per home, and you can add another $100 for drainage flashing at the joint between the floor and the wall. And usually, no bling bling, no go.

1. POURED CONCRETE WALLS

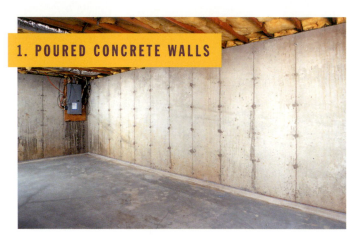

- Most common today.

2. CONCRETE BLOCK WALLS

- Most common from 1940 to 1975.
- Still used today.

3. STONE WALLS

- Common in older homes.

4. WOOD FOUNDATION WALLS

- Treated wood stud walls and plywood.
- Very rare in most areas.

5. MONOLITHIC FOUNDATIONS

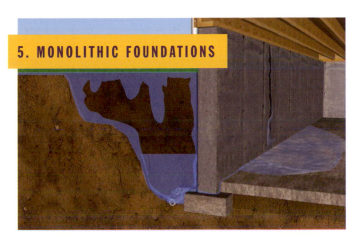

- Could be block or poured walls.
- The difference is that the floor and footing are poured in one piece.
- With the walls on top, it's a two-piece foundation instead of a three-piece.

6. PRECAST FOUNDATION WALLS

- Newest idea, still relatively rare.

Janesky's First Law of Hydrodynamics

WATER FLOWS DOWNHILL

Dirt Around a Foundation Settles

After construction, loose soil — called backfill — is used to fill the hole around a home's foundation. The soil will settle, especially in the first few years, and this settling doesn't help a wet basement situation. Dirt should be added so that water does not flow toward the foundation. Unlike dirt, mulch is porous and water easily passes through it, so mulch doesn't count.

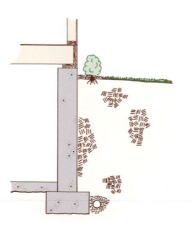

HOUSE AGE: 3 Months

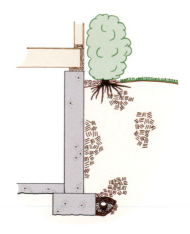

HOUSE AGE: 7 Years

ANYTHING BUT AVERAGE

It's no secret that wet weather floods basements — but dry weather is a part of the problem, too. In periods of drought, the soil shrinks away from the foundation, leaving voids for the next rain to easily flow down into your basement. Average rainfall means an average of wet periods and dry periods. A low average rainfall is no guarantee of a dry basement.

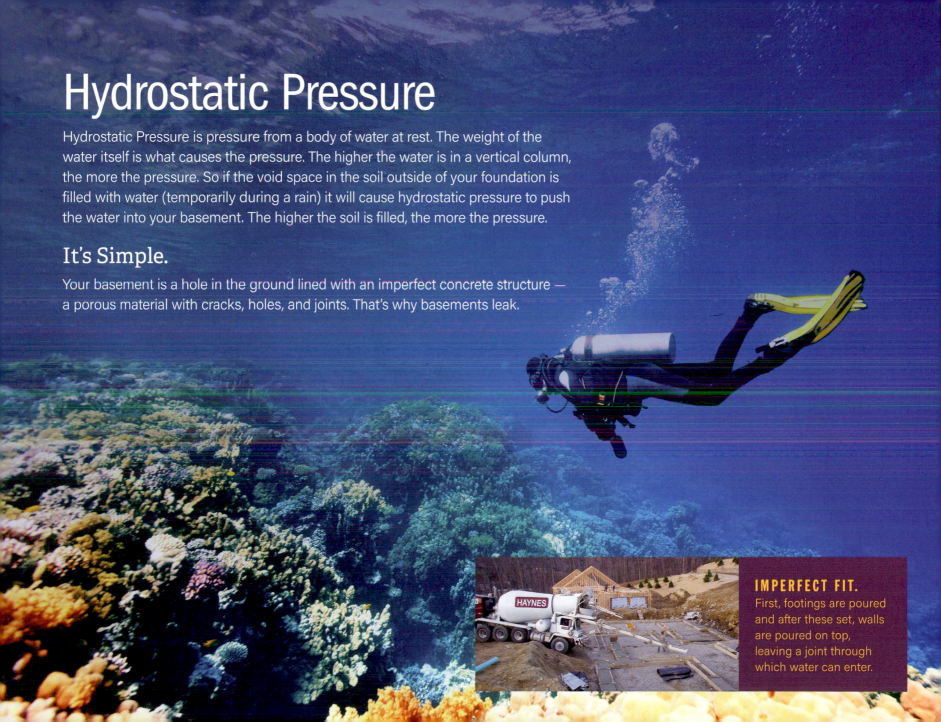

Hydrostatic Pressure

Hydrostatic Pressure is pressure from a body of water at rest. The weight of the water itself is what causes the pressure. The higher the water is in a vertical column, the more the pressure. So if the void space in the soil outside of your foundation is filled with water (temporarily during a rain) it will cause hydrostatic pressure to push the water into your basement. The higher the soil is filled, the more the pressure.

It's Simple.

Your basement is a hole in the ground lined with an imperfect concrete structure — a porous material with cracks, holes, and joints. That's why basements leak.

IMPERFECT FIT.
First, footings are poured and after these set, walls are poured on top, leaving a joint through which water can enter.

CHAPTER THREE

OUTER LIMITS
What Can (or Should) Be Done Outside

One way to fix a wet basement is to dig up the earth outside around your foundation, waterproof the walls and install a new footing drain. This is almost never a good option. Why?

First of all, you'll be replacing the same system that failed you — and how long will it last this time? The big problem is the excavation itself. You have to dig down to the bottom of the footing, about 8 feet. Picture standing in a trench, looking up at where the grass used to be. An 8-foot deep trench has to be at least 8 feet wide at the top (12 feet if you ask OSHA).

And where will all that dirt that comes out of the hole go? It's piled up in the rest of your yard. You can expect about 25 feet of your yard all the way around your home to be destroyed.

Everything in this area must be removed, including porches, driveways, sidewalks, landscaping, air conditioning units, decks, steps and so on. Then after the work is done, the dirt that was excavated — which is now fluffed up and loose on your lawn — is put back in the trench. It will take years for this dirt to settle, and as it does, new dirt must be added against the foundation to keep the slope away from the house. Then you can put your driveway, sidewalks, decks, porches, and landscaping back. This is reason enough not to consider doing the job outside.

If you need more reasons to dismiss this dastardly idea, how about these:

1. **Where will the drain go to?** If you don't have a lot of slope on your property to take the pipe out to daylight, then you need to bring the pipe inside the foundation to a sump pump anyway. Exterior excavation does not address water vapor coming through your basement walls and floor. This method does not address humidity, nor does it ensure that mold won't grow. What if something goes wrong and there is still a little seepage? What will you do then? Dig it all up again? Outside systems are not serviceable.

2. **It costs a lot of money** — like up to $20,000 to go all the way around your home!

I think we can close the book on this option.

Grading

If the soil around your home is pitched toward the foundation, it's a good idea to add dirt so that the ground slopes away. Be sure not to use sand or mulch, because water flows right down through these materials, whether they are pitched or not. It's best to use clay or other dense dirt.

Be sure that you keep the dirt at least four inches below the siding, though. If the siding is close to or touching the soil, it will rot, and then you'll have another problem. Termites could also use wood siding to create a highway from the soil into your home undetected.

Don't rely on grading alone to keep your basement dry.

Gutters

Keep your gutters clean. There are a variety of gutter screening and cover materials that work well to keep them free of leaves and debris.

DON'T RELY ON CLEAN GUTTERS ALONE TO KEEP YOUR BASEMENT DRY.

Downspouts

You didn't need to read a book to have someone tell you to keep your gutters from dumping water next to your foundation, did you? I only have to say it so someone doesn't say my book is incomplete without this obvious advice? There are a few options to laying ugly pipes and contraptions across your lawn that get in the way of mowing and your annual croquet game at the family picnic.

One way is to bury pipes underground to the edge of the yard to take the roof water away. However, you need pitch (a downward slope) on your yard to do it. And remember, all the leaves and pine needles and acorns and twigs that wind up in your gutter will be going into those underground pipes. If you do bury pipes underground I recommend you avoid using elbows and put as much pitch on the pipe as possible.

There are a few other options that work very well. An underground extension called LawnScape Outlet enables downspout water to escape with virtually no pitch. It's also extremely popular for discharge lines on sump pumps! Another product called RainChute is recessed into the ground just an inch or so and takes the water up to 7 feet away. Usually this is all you need to make a big difference. Unlike an above-ground pipe, RainChute does not create an unsightlly tripping or mowing hazard, yet it is not underground either so it's not expensive and won't clog.

For areas that are landscaped and don't need mowing, a simple extension called RainChute EZ will do the trick.

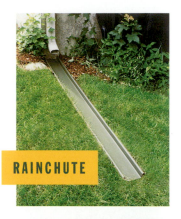

RAINCHUTE

RAINCHUTE EZ

LAWNSCAPE OUTLET

"Curtain Drains" & Yard Drainage

The layman may suggest a curtain drain to cure your wet basement woes. Whoa! This **won't** work.

A curtain drain is a trench some distance from your foundation that has a pipe in it and is filled with crushed stone. Sometimes the trench will be filled to the top, appearing as a stripe of stone in your yard. This type of drain is often used on sloping lots, on the uphill side of a building. It makes sense as a method to intercept water coming down the hill, but cannot be relied upon to protect a basement from water problems.

Other types of shallow drains in a yard can only be relied upon to prevent puddling in the yard and not to prevent a basement from leaking. We have plenty of customers who drained their bank accounts with their local backhoe owner to no avail.

In and Out

Beware of waterproofing contractors who say they will do two drains, one outside and one inside. They tell you it's better because the outside drain will stop the water from coming through your foundation in the first place — but why then do they need an inside system? Most customers are led to believe the outside drain will be very deep; and it seems to make sense. But in reality the installers just dig a trench 12 inches deep or so, and when they come to an obstacle like a porch or driveway they stop the trench and start again on the other side of the obstacle. The outside drain is useless.

The whole idea of drains inside and out is window dressing to justify high prices for what they are providing.

Many people, including me, think it's a scam.

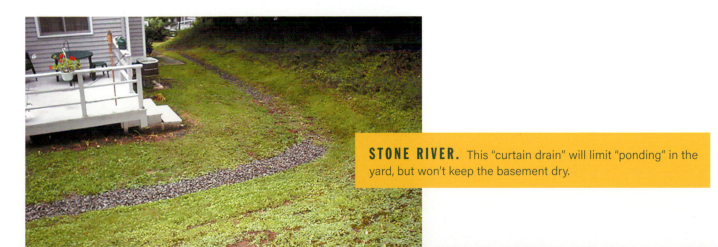

STONE RIVER. This "curtain drain" will limit "ponding" in the yard, but won't keep the basement dry.

CHAPTER FOUR

INSIDER'S STRATEGY
Drainage Systems That Work

If digging outside is not the answer, what is? Digging on the inside! Jackhammering, to be more specific. By installing a drainage system around the inside of the basement along the wall, you can capture water at the most common point of entry – the floor/wall joint. You can also capture water that penetrates the walls, and prevent the center of the floor from leaking by intercepting the water at the perimeter of the floor before it gets to the center.

The advantages of an interior drainage system include:

1. It can be installed without digging a massive trench in your yard

2. Installation takes only a day or two

3. It is easily serviceable year-round

4. It works

Even in basements that are already finished, it's still much easier to waterproof from the inside than the outside. Most full-time basement waterproofing companies offer interior drainage systems. Some are old-fashioned and generic, and others are modern and specially designed for the job.

In the 1950s and before, clay pipe sections about 18 inches long were used for underground and under-floor drains. There were no holes in the pipe, but instead the sections were laid with a ¼-inch space between them to let in water. Since the pipe sections were made from clay — like a chimney flue pipe or a brick — they called it drain "tile." This term is still used today to refer to a pipe with holes or slots in it that is buried for drainage, even though the industry switched to plastic pipe long ago. These generic, round, perforated drainpipes can be used for field drainage, exterior footing drains, road drainage, and just about anything.

OLD FASHIONED. Clay "tile" pipe.

Clay or plastic, the pipe was usually laid alongside the footing in new construction applications, and many contractors do the same for retrofitting an existing home. However, this placement of the pipe isn't necessarily the best. Existing drains alongside the footing have failed — usually by clogging with dirt. In the 1960s and afterward, new methods began to be developed. Today, a system called WaterGuard, developed in 1994, has proven to have all the benefits that homeowners and contractors are looking for.

WaterGuard is engineered specifically to be an efficient, long-lasting interior perimeter basement waterproofing system. The big difference is that the WaterGuard sits on top of the footing, instead of alongside it. This is important because it keeps the wet dirt (commonly referred to as mud) from getting into the drain because the drain does not sit in the mud.

Requirements of a Good Interior Drainage System

- Designed not to clog — sits on top of the footing

- Has a built-in ⅜-inch gap between the floor and the wall to drain wall leaks

- Does not rely on filter fabric

- Has a big drain outlet to the sump

- Will not cause structural damage to the foundation

WaterGuard meets all these requirements. With a sub-floor system such as WaterGuard, an experienced installer can make various modifications to account for unusual foundation situations.

The Self-Flushing Lie

If anyone explains to you that their pipe is "self-flushing," flush them from the competition to earn your business. To say such a thing implies that mud gets in but will be flushed out. Where did the mud come from? What's there after it gets "washed away" by the drainage system? Where does it go — into the sump hole to clog it up? Some contractors will take corrugated pipe (the cheapest of them all) and say the corrugations (which are not spirals) cause a spiraling action to self-clean the pipe. This is a lie.

Another lie that's told sometimes is that parts of the floor must be left in place to prevent the walls from collapsing. If this were true, millions of homes would have fallen down by now.

Unfortunately, the basement waterproofing industry has lots of characters who will say just about anything to make their pitch sound good to you and to discredit their competitors. Think about the statements that the salespeople are making. If you smell a rat, there probably is one.

Deeper Is Not Better

If a drainage system is too deep, not only does it have a greater risk of clogging, but soil from underneath the foundation can wash into it and leave voids, which can cause settling of your foundation. In addition, by trying to keep the water level much lower than necessary, you will be pumping out more water. Your pump could run all the time, and the discharge water will keep the surface of your yard wet all the time.

The Great Shape Debate

Some waterproofing companies make a big deal over the shape of their pipe. The fact is that when you buy a drainage system you are not buying pipe, but a space for water to flow in. The water doesn't care about the shape of the space. The important question is where the space is, and whether it's set up to take in water and not mud.

The Alarmist?

I don't want to join the ranks of those who say the sky will fall if you do something wrong. To my knowledge, no basement waterproofer has ever killed a customer. The sun always comes up tomorrow. This is not life-or-death we're talking about. The worst that could happen is that you wind up paying a lot of money to have something fixed in your home and then have to do it all over again a few years later. I don't want to sound like an alarmist with warnings of what not to do. It's your home, your money and your decision. I am going to give you information to help eliminate the chances of your wasting any effort and money, and to help you get your whole basement very dry, all the time.

The In-the-Mud Out-of-the-Mud Debate

Will all systems alongside the footing clog? No. But many will. Some soon, some later, some never. It depends on the soil and foundation conditions and the water problem. With the WaterGuard system, you will not have to worry about the system clogging — and how many times do you want to have your basement waterproofed, anyway?

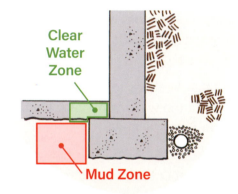

Clear Water Zone

Mud Zone

UP ABOVE IT. Systems that sit in the mud can become part of the mud. Systems that sit above the mud will stay above it.

The Floor/Wall Joint

Open for Business

One key to a waterproofing system is that it must have an opening to drain water from the walls. Wall leaks, now or in the future, include leaks from wall cracks, pipe penetrations, flooding window wells, condensation, and other sources. Of course, we want to fix all the leaks we see with the original installation, but we should also address leaks that may come up later. A gap at the edge of the floor will catch any leaks, prevent the floor from getting wet, and prevent damage to anything that is on the floor.

This gap is sometimes called a French drain, although those who know a little commonly use this term to mean different things. The gap along the wall can be made by sticking a piece of wood between the floor and wall, concreting up to it, and pulling it out. This makes a big ugly gap that can fill up with debris from the floor.

A better way is to have spacers along the backside of a flange that sticks up above the floor. The optimum size for this gap is ⅜ inch. You want it to function and look nice and neat — as if it's supposed to be there.

Beware of systems that say they have a flange that is tight to the wall and yet takes water from the wall. If you have your first grade diploma, you know that's impossible.

CATCH-ALL. A French drain-style wall gap will catch water from the wall, as well as dirt and debris from the basement floor.

A BETTER WAY. WaterGuard flange spacers make a nice neat finished look and kep dirt and debris from the floor out of the gap.

Beware of Filter Fabrics

Inside or outside, systems that use filter fabrics clog, slowing the flow rate down considerably. Think about the word filter. What filter doesn't clog? And when it does, how are you going to replace a filter under your basement floor?

Two Stage Waterproofing

A typical waterproofing system installation involves removing the perimeter of the floor to install a drain. However, a monolithic type foundation is a floor with thick edges to it, and since those thick edges are the structural footing of the house, it cannot be removed.

The **Two Stage Waterproofing System** keeps the basement dry without risk of structural foundation issues.

A **DryTrak® System** is installed along the wall to capture seepage from walls and the floor wall joint, and drains into a sub-floor drainage system which protects against floor leaks, and drains to a sump pump system.

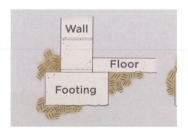

A **conventionally constructed foundation** is three pieces – footing, wall, and floor.

When they leak, our WaterGuard® draining system is the perfect solution.

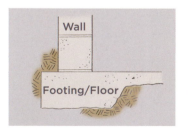

But a **monolithic foundation** is constructed in two pieces – a floor and footing are poured together, and the wall is built on top. Because the perimeter of the floor is a foot or more thick and it is the structural member bearing the weight of the whole house to the ground, it should not be removed.

DRAIN TRENCH INSTALLED

DRAIN PIPES INSTALLED

DRYTRAK® INSTALLED

FLOOR RE-CONCRETED

Expect Dust

As doctors tell patients who are about to have an operation: It gets worse before it gets better. But in the case of your home having its water problem fixed, it only gets worse for a day or two. Jackhammering in a home is loud. Take the young and old out to the park the morning of the installation. It's also dusty. How dusty? Not very dusty at all if your basement floor is soft and damp. If your floor is hard and thick, you'll get more dust. Will that dust get upstairs? Maybe some will. On a windy day, it will. Plan on cleaning the house the day after the installation. In most homes, it's not necessary.

Doorways and Stairways to the Outside

If you have a doorway or stairway that leads to the outside, you'll want to have a trench drain installed in front of it while you are having your waterproofing system installed. A trench drain is a half-round pipe with a grate that fits on top of it. The grate is flush or slightly below the floor to catch any water that may enter from the outside. It's easy to convert between WaterGuard and trench drain along the perimeter of your floor.

This way you are protected against leakage from a hatchway door, a sliding door, or even a garage door. Even if your door currently doesn't leak, with the right snow, slush or heavy rain conditions, it can. It doesn't cost any more to add the trench drain if you are having a WaterGuard system installed.

Water Heater Leaks

Whether the water in your basement is from a groundwater leak or from a plumbing leak, the results are the same — with the exception that your homeowner's insurance will cover the damage from the plumbing leak. In fact, the number one type of claim that insurance companies pay out on homeowner's policies is water damage. One of the top claims of water damage is from water heaters leaking.

Water heaters don't last very long. During the life of a home the water heater will be replaced many times, and a common way that a water heater lets you know that it needs to be replaced is by leaking. When a water heater leaks it doesn't just empty out, it continues to leak because it continues to automatically refill itself. So it could leak for weeks if you don't notice. I have seen basements with many inches of water from water heater leaks.

Here's What to Do for Water Heater Leaks – *Get FloodRing*

A product called FloodRing can be easily installed around your water heater. This 4-inch-high ring gets sealed to the floor, contains water heater leakage, and drains it to the perimeter drainage system that your waterproofing contractor will install. It doesn't cost much, and will one day pay for itself many times over.

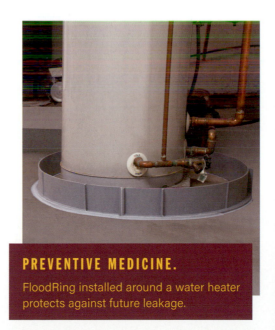

PREVENTIVE MEDICINE.
FloodRing installed around a water heater protects against future leakage.

Radon Gas

Radon is a naturally occurring radioactive gas that comes from radium deposits in the earth's crust. If present in the soil under your home, it can find its way in via the basement or crawl space

Don't panic. It's relatively common and easy to get rid of.

Some people think that basement waterproofing and radon reduction systems are incompatible. While it's true that gaps, cracks, and holes in the basement floor and walls need to be sealed as part of the strategy to get rid of radon, this can be done without compromising the waterproofing system.

With products described in this book and proper air sealing, your Basement Systems dealer can help make your home radon free.

CHAPTER FIVE

UP AND AWAY

Sump Pumps – Better Than Ever

Everyone knows the myth of Sisyphus, sentenced by Zeus to roll a heavy boulder up a hill in Hades. Every time he got almost to the top, the rock would slip from his grasp and roll back to the bottom. He was doomed to almost solve his problem, time and again.

Don't be like Sisyphus, setting up a system to move water away from your basement, but not far enough. Don't almost solve your wet basement problem. Solve it completely by pumping the water far, far away.

Now that you've channeled all groundwater that used to leak in from around the perimeter of your basement, you need to find a way to get rid of it. You can either use a pipe to carry the water away by gravity (downhill) to daylight, or use a sump pump to pump it up and out.

Gravity drains require that you have a substantial slope on your property so you can dig a trench from underneath your foundation to daylight while having the pipe pitch ⅛ inch per foot (one foot of pitch for every 100 feet you go out away from the house). Most homes don't have that kind of pitch on their property. To get a trench that deep and go that far can also be a big mess and cause substantial disturbance to other things outside your home. And remember your neighbors probably won't talk to you at this year's block party if you discharge your drainage directly onto their property.

If gravity drains are easy to do on your property, it's not a bad option. But you must keep them from getting clogged, frozen or having the end covered over with ice or leaves and debris. For those who do choose this option, I would recommend that a sump pump with an alarm be installed inside as a backup in case anything ever goes wrong with the gravity drain.

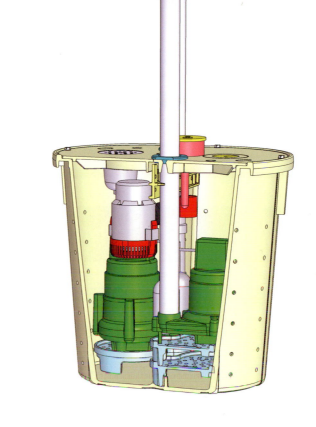

For 99.9% of us, a sump pump is our best option. Despite any stories you have heard over the years about folks getting flooded because their sump pump was on the blink again, today's sump equipment is better than ever and very reliable — unless you cheap out and just buy a basic pump-in-a-hole. Then you'll end up telling a tale of woe one day about your pump failing and causing your basement to flood.

Pumps and Switches

When we say "sump," we mean the hole in the floor. The pump that goes in the sump is very important. There are different kinds of pumps that will perform differently and have shorter or longer expected lifetimes. I'll make it simple for you:

PUMPS / **SWITCHES**	What is *NOT* Recommended	Why
PUMPS	**Pedestal pumps that stick up above the floor.**	You can't install them in an airtight sump, low capacity
PUMPS	**Plastic pumps**	They hold heat in and burn out faster, lower quality
PUMPS	**Pumps with screened inlets**	Screens clog easily, choking flow
PUMPS	**¼ hp pumps**	Too small
SWITCHES	**"Ball on a wire" switches**	They need a big area to swing and can get hung up
SWITCHES	**Pressure switches**	They aren't as precise, and "on level" can change over time

Automatic pump switches are vital, too. The best pump in the world needs an excellent switch to tell it when to turn on and when to turn off.

What *IS* Recommended	Why
Cast Iron Pumps	They are quiet, cool well, and last longer
Mechanical float switches (float on a rod)	They're reliable, with positive on and off levels

Based on these criteria, I recommend Zoeller pumps. We have used them for years after brief stints with other pumps, and the results are very clear.

Pump, Don't Swirl

Many manufacturers and dealers lie about how many gallons their pumps can remove per hour to make them sound better than other companies' products. The most common way they get away with misleading folks is to quote how many gallons their pumps will move in an hour at a very low "head." Head is a term meaning how high you pump the water. If you pump it 2 feet up out of the sump hole, and 7 feet over your basement wall, that's a 9-foot head. The higher the head, the lower the volume of water a pump can push.

Some companies quote how much water their pumps will pump at a 3-foot head. Who only has to pump water 3 feet high? This is totally irrelevant. Many even say "up to x gallons per hour," when this number is at zero head! Who needs to pump water at zero head? The water is already there — you don't have to pump it! They should say, "Will swirl water around a sump hole at 3500 gallons per hour." This is a misrepresentation of the highest order.

An AC pump that moves over 2000 gallons per hour at an 8-foot head is a good, strong pump.

THE PUMP IS ONLY **PART** OF A

Sump Pump System

Besides the pump, there are other elements of a good sump pump system that are very important.

Lifetime Warranty?

No pump manufacturer gives a lifetime warranty on their pumps, and there is a good reason. A lifetime warranty doesn't make a pump better. Some irresponsible contractors will tell you there is such a warranty on their pump — "free replacements forever" — to seduce you to buy their whole solution. This is irresponsible. Ask yourself, "How do I know when to call to get my free replacement?" The answer is when your basement is flooded — and that's what this entire book is trying to prevent, as well as what you spent your money to stop from happening. The damage will be done, and the 10-year, 20-year or lifetime warranty won't help you.

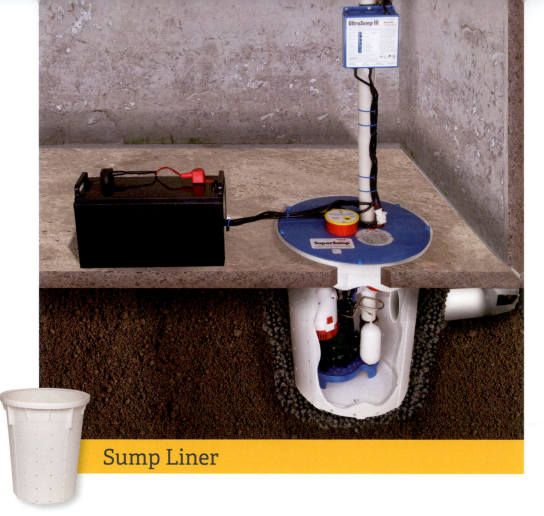

Sump Liner

You don't want your pump to clog up in a muddy hole in the floor. And you don't want it in a 5-gallon bucket that doesn't hold a lot of water and will cause the pump to "short-cycle" (go on and off very quickly). Instead, you should have a sturdy liner or housing for your sump pump with holes in it to accept water directly from the ground as well as a larger inlet hole to allow your perimeter drainage system to empty into it. There should be about 100 ⅜-inch holes in it. The liner should be about 2 feet deep and 18 inches wide, and have a rim that accepts a sealed cover.

Airtight Sump Lid

The sump should have an airtight lid to prevent water from evaporating into your basement, to stop stuff from falling and clogging the pump, and to quiet the system. Depending on the cover, it can also make the installation look good. Instead of a necessary evil in your home, you should have a thoughtfully engineered system.

Pump Stand

A CleanPump stand will elevate the pump above the bottom of the sump liner a bit, allowing for some sediment, mud, debris, or gravel to settle to the bottom without clogging or otherwise affecting the pump. It also keeps the check valve and discharge pipe clean. A check valve (one-way valve) should be installed on all sump pump discharge lines, so that when the pump shuts off the water in the pipe doesn't flow back into the sump hole, to be pumped again on the next cycle.

Floor Drain in Sump Lid

Not if, but when you have a plumbing leak and the water floods out onto the basement floor, you'll want to use your sump hole to drain the water away. With an airtight lid, the water will fill up your basement. (Unlike groundwater leaks, plumbing leaks and the damage they cause might be covered by your homeowner's insurance.) Putting a floor drain in the sump lid is the answer. But wait, won't a sump drain allow water vapor to evaporate into my basement? Not with Basement Systems' airtight floor drain. This places a specially designed cup and ball underneath the floor drain which allows water to go down, but doesn't allow air to come up.

Pump Alarm

How would you know if your sump pump had failed and you were in danger of being flooded? Unless you have an alarm, the answer is, when your basement is already flooded, which is just what you are trying to avoid. A battery-powered alarm that sounds automatically when the water reaches a level above the point where the pump(s) should normally turn on is essential. The patented WaterWatch alarm does just that, telling you there is a problem before the floor gets wet, so you have a chance to do something about it.

All Too Common

Low on performance, hard on the eyes.
It doesn't have to be this way...

Form + Function

A Sump Pump as Art!

What if my pump fails?
What if the power goes out?

These are questions you should be asking yourself. After all, you want your whole basement dry all the time, right? Well, you're not going to get that if you don't plan on...

- the power going out one day — which usually happens in a big storm with rain
- the pump coming unplugged
- the circuit breaker tripping
- the primary pump failing
- the primary pump not being able to keep up with the amount of water in a very heavy rain

Remember all the stories of woe people have told you about getting flooded when their sump pump failed? These are the reasons behind those failures. You don't have to go through that if you have the right equipment.

The King (and Queens) of Sump Pumps

1 + 1 = 1

If you have more than one AC pump to get more water out in a big rain, it makes no sense to hook them up to one discharge pipe. Using the "ten pounds of stuff in a five-pound bag" logic, you can't get more water out with two pumps unless you have two discharge pipes to the outside.

The TripleSafe twin liner, lids, CleanPump stands, bridge, etc., are all specially engineered to work together.

The answer is a system called the TripleSafe sump pump system. This top-of-the-line system sports three sump pumps in one sump liner. Pump 1 is a high-quality Zoeller ⅓ hp pump and will do the lion's share of the pumping very efficiently most of the time. Pump 2 is a ½ hp Zoeller pump, set a bit higher in the sump hole, that turns on in the event that the first pump fails or can't keep up. This second pump is more powerful and has a separate discharge line to give you that "turbo boost" in the rare cases when you need it.

Pump 3 is a DC (battery-operated) UltraSump pump that kicks in if the power goes out. It is available with one or two specially designed maintenance-free batteries to pump out over 12,000 or 24,000 gallons of water respectively at an 8-foot head.

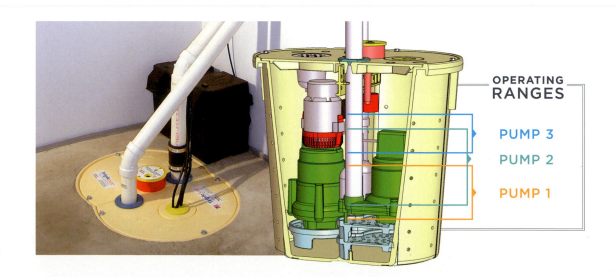

OPERATING RANGES

PUMP 3

PUMP 2

PUMP 1

Importance of a Backup Pumping System

It is important to note that there are many kinds of backup systems provided. I just saw one with a contractor price of $79, which he would put together with a $50 car battery and sell for $400 to $800. When it comes to backup equipment, the variance of quality is a chasm. The low-end equipment most often will not work when you need it. And the folks like you who buy backup pumping equipment really need and want the protection.

To give you an example, nearly all suppliers of backup equipment do not supply batteries. Batteries are heavy and expensive and difficult to ship. Instead, they leave it to the contractor to go to the automotive store and buy a car battery. Car batteries are not made for this application. Their ampere-hour capacity diminishes quickly after a year in this application and they will not get the "gallonage" out of your basement when you need them to.

Other suppliers provide expensive backup pumping systems with batteries that need maintenance every six months. If you don't remember, you are out of luck. Sealed, maintenance-free batteries are the only sensible option.

Float switches are extremely important, too. The best pump in the world needs to have a switch to tell it when to go on and off.

Many primary and backup pump systems come with a tethered float switch — a "ball-on-a-wire" design. These have to swing up and down to operate. They commonly get hung up — and cause a flood.

No pump or backup pump is perfect. But so many are really pitiful protection. That's why Basement Systems' TripleSafe and UltraSump are specifically engineered to do what we need them to, and offer redundancy.

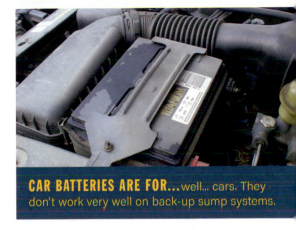

CAR BATTERIES ARE FOR...well... cars. They don't work very well on back-up sump systems.

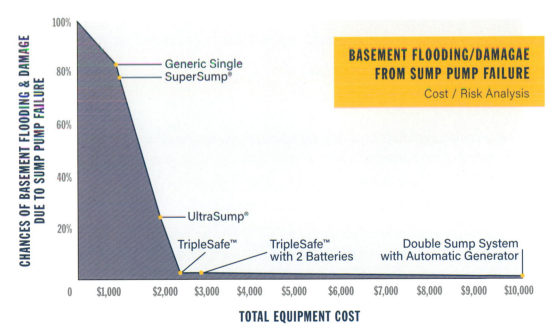

BASEMENT FLOODING/DAMAGAE FROM SUMP PUMP FAILURE

Cost / Risk Analysis

Generic Single SuperSump®

UltraSump®

TripleSafe™

TripleSafe™ with 2 Batteries

Double Sump System with Automatic Generator

CHANCES OF BASEMENT FLOODING & DAMAGE DUE TO SUMP PUMP FAILURE

100%
80%
60%
40%
20%

0   $1,000 $2,000 $3,000 $4,000 $5,000 $6,000 $7,000 $8,000 $9,000 $10,000

TOTAL EQUIPMENT COST

Calculating How Much Battery Backup Protection You are Buying

A simple equation can tell you how many gallons your DC equipment can pump out of your basement when the power goes out. Gallons out equals ampere-hour capacity of the battery divided by DC amperage of the pump times gallons-per-hour (gph) rating of the pump at an 8-foot head.

In the case of Basement Systems UltraSump:

Gal. out *(liters out)* = amp-hours of battery / DC amps of pump x gph *(LPH)*

Gal. out *(liters out)* = 120 amp-hours / 19.8 amps x 2010 gph *(5676 L)*

Gal. out *(liters out)* = 6.06 x 2010 *(5676 L)*

Gal. out *(liters out)* = 12,181 *(43,956 L)*

This calculation assumes you are pumping the water 8 feet high and that the battery is new. As batteries age, they lose some of their ampere-hour capacity. Because of these and other factors, we usually understate the performance.

A special unit called an UltraSump Dual Battery Switching Unit allows two batteries to be hooked up, doubling the number of gallons the backup pump will pump out.

Everyone asks "How long will the pump last?" We can't answer this question because it is the wrong question. How long your battery-powered backup pump will last in a power outage depends upon how hard it rains when the power is out and how much water is in the ground under your particular home. One thing is for sure, 12,181 gallons of water is a lot of water. It's the average size of a basement, filled to the ceiling!

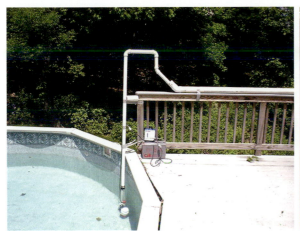

An entire pool? Can an UltraSump with a 120-amp battery pump out a 9000-gallon swimming pool at an 8-foot head?

You betcha! On a single battery, the UltraSump emptied the pool and was raring to attack the pond in back.

Is a Generator an Option?

A generator is a good idea if you have an automatic one permanently installed that senses when the power goes out and starts up automatically. It needs to be wired by an electrician. A typical generator can be hooked up to run your sump pump, a few lights, the furnace and the fridge. This costs between $7,000 and $10,000 in most cases. If you go this route, be sure to install two AC primary pumps to cover you in case of pump failure, as a generator only eliminates the need for the DC backup pump.

You can purchase a portable generator for $400 or so. However, you must be home (and awake) to notice when the power fails. Then you must drag the generator outside, gas it up, start it up, and run an extension cord to your sump pump. This is not a good option.

Electrical Outlets

Electrical outlets are usually not included in your waterproofing contractor's scope of work. Although your waterproofer will leave with your sumps operational, plan on having an electrician wire a proper outlet at the sump location right after the waterproofer is done.

If you have more than one AC pump (as with a TripleSafe system), two outlets on two different circuits will ensure that you still have one AC pump operational if a circuit breaker trips.

Alternate Power Sources?

Some alternate backup power sources for sump pumps appeared on the market in recent years, and they sounded great at first.

One is a backup battery power system for a single AC-operated pump. When the power goes out, the system converts the DC power to AC power and runs your only sump pump. The manufacturer will tell you that it's better, since your AC-operated unit will pump more than a DC-operated one. This is true, but not a key issue in most cases. The main issue here is that you have only one pump. If the pump fails, you get flooded despite this backup protection. Secondly, converting DC to AC power is very inefficient. You lose more than half your power in the process. Your pump will run and pump plenty of water out, but not for long. In our test, it only lasted one hour, and then the batteries went dead. Since the primary pump we used pumped 2200 gallons an hour, this system offered only 2200 gallons of protection.

Another single-pump system uses a DC-operated pump with batteries hooked up to it. When the power is on, the AC current is converted to DC to run the pump. When the power is off, the pump runs on the batteries. Sounds good. But you only have one pump, and if it fails you're dead in the water. In addition, no matter how strong the DC pump, the amount of water you'll pump will depend on the amount of battery power you put into it.

CAUTION: Winter can be hazardous to your basement's health.

Freezing Discharge Lines

Your sump pump gets the water out of the basement and away from your house with a pipe — usually plastic and usually about 1½ inches in diameter. This pipe runs on the surface of the ground, or in a shallow buried trench, and discharges the water onto the surface away from the house.

The problem is that in winter the outlet of the pipe becomes blocked with snow and ice. When the pump runs, it fills the pipe with water. (Ten feet of 1½-inch pipe holds one gallon of water). Since the water can't get out of the pipe due to the ice at the outlet, the whole pipe fills with water and freezes. Now your pump runs, but cannot get the water out, and your basement floods. Just what you were trying to avoid!

Basement Systems has a solution—the IceGuard system. This is a specially engineered fitting that goes outside your home and automatically ejects the water away from the exterior wall in the event that the pipe freezes. It is designed with holes to allow this to happen, yet no water at all gets out of these openings when the pipe is not frozen.

SNOW, NO PROBLEM.
The patented IceGuard solves the problem of frozen discharge lines.

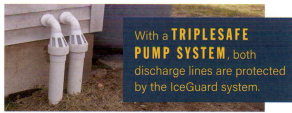

With a **TRIPLESAFE PUMP SYSTEM**, both discharge lines are protected by the IceGuard system.

A Real Dog

Beware of contractors who use a roof drain contraption with slots all the way around, and try to pass it off as a protection against frozen discharge lines. Because water dribbles along the slots (spilling next to the foundation) when the pump runs, the fitting freezes up and closes off the escape openings.

A lot of discussion about sump pumps and pump-related issues — right? Well, you said you wanted your basement dry all the time!

The short answer is to get a TripleSafe sump pump system with two discharge lines protected by the IceGuard sump pump discharge line system.

Now you're safe.

Why didn't I just tell you that first?

CHAPTER SIX

IMPORTANT | **ORGANIC = MOLD FOOD.** Wood, drywall, and latex paint only serve as mold breeding grounds in the basement environment.

BASEMENT DANDRUFF. Paint and wall coatings only flake off over time — even if they read "special for basements" on the can.

GOING VERTICAL

Basement Walls You Can Love

OK now, get up off the floor — and look at your basement walls. I'm betting that they are not very attractive. Almost certainly they are letting cold and moisture into your home. You probably wouldn't mind an upgrade. The good news is that there are a number of excellent choices, depending on your circumstances (and preferences). In this chapter, I'll help you decide which of them is right for you.

Once you have drained water away at the perimeter of your basement floor and made sure it's pumped out reliably, the next thing you'll want to think about is your basement walls. You can get the floor dry without doing anything to the walls — but is that what you want?

Your basement walls allow water vapor to pass through them. Block walls not only allow lots of water vapor through because of their hollow core, but cold (and damp) outside air passes through them easily. And air, water and water vapor can pass through stone walls.

Look at your basement walls. Chances are they are damp, stained, chalky, flaky and ugly. Ask yourself if you are happy with them. Chances are the answer is no. So, what can you have done?

There are a few options, including coatings, paneling and vapor barriers.

Wall Coatings

Coatings are not a good option simply because they don't stay on the wall for a very long time. This is because the water and water vapor are already through the wall by the time they get to the coatings and push the coating off the wall. When the coating begins to peel and flake, the wall looks worse than it did in the first place.

Five Good Options

There are five good options for what do to with your basement walls. Choosing the best one depends upon what you are doing with your basement.

If you . . .

- are looking for a finished look without fully finishing your basement, then **ZenWall** paneling is best.
- are leaving your basement unfinished, then **BrightWall** paneling is best.
- are "conventionally" finishing your basement, then use **Basement to Beautiful** panels or **Foamax**
- have stone walls, then **CleanSpace** is best

Is your basement already finished? And needs to be waterproofed?

NO PROBLEM!

The EverLast finished wall restoration system is the perfect solution. By removing just the bottom of your walls (getting rid of the damaged, smelly part) we gain access to do the waterproofing right — and then we can save the undamaged upper walls. Finally, the bottom of the wall is restored using inorganic (mold-proof) materials that won't be damaged if you have a flood from a plumbing leak.

ZenWall Paneling

The revolutionary ZenWall basement paneling system is a ¼ inch-thick encapsulated fiberglass core with a reflective foil vapor barrier on the back side and a decorative vinyl finish on the front side. It is used with a perimeter basement waterproofing system to waterproof a basement wall and stop vapor from coming through the wall into the basement air.

The finish on ZenWall looks great — about as great as you can get without doing a full basement finishing project — for a fraction of the price. It makes a huge difference in what your basement looks like and how it feels to spend time there.

ZenWall panels are a revolutionary option for basement walls. Simply put, ZenWall panels are the simplest, easiest way to waterproof your basement walls and get a finished look.

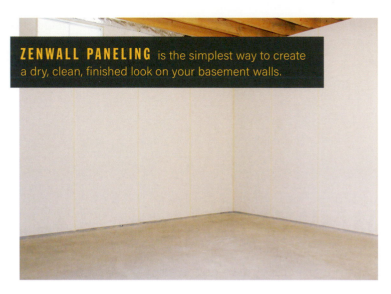

ZENWALL PANELING is the simplest way to create a dry, clean, finished look on your basement walls.

Inorganic? Yes! All the materials in ZenWall will not support mold — perfect for a basement.

BrightWall Paneling

Think of it as a plastic version of Formica. The BrightWall system uses semi-rigid white plastic panels installed on your basement walls with drilled-in white fasteners. It can never come off your walls no matter how much dampness comes through.

BrightWall paneling drains any water leaks down behind it to the (WaterGuard) perimeter drainage system without you ever knowing it. It also stops water vapor from coming through the walls and evaporating into your basement.

While not as nice looking as ZenWall, BrightWall really dresses up your unfinished basement for about 30% less! BrightWall looks great and makes the basement much brighter.

BRIGHTWALL PANELING stops water vapor from permeating basement walls and drains water down to a perimeter drainage system (WaterGuard) if necessary. Plus, it looks great and really brightens a basement!

CleanSpace Wall System

We use CleanSpace, a heavy, durable plastic liner (like a pool liner) for lining dirt crawl spaces. It is perfect as a wall solution for stone wall basements. Because stone walls are not flat, they are not candidates for ZenWall or BrightWall paneling. CleanSpace provides a vapor barrier, drains water behind it and dramatically brightens the basement. It will have little waves in it because it comes off a roll rather than in panels, but is very durable and nearly impossible to rip.

The solution to damp and leaking stone walls. The CleanSpace wall system stops water vapor, drains wall leaks, and brightens your basement — especially effective in basements with stone walls.

Foamax

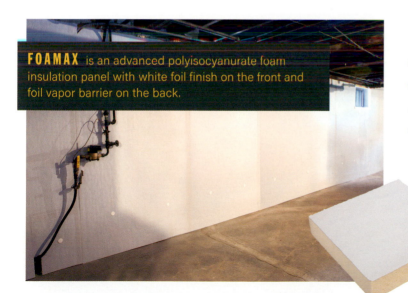

FOAMAX is an advanced polyisocyanurate foam insulation panel with white foil finish on the front and foil vapor barrier on the back.

Cold basement walls make cold basements in winter, and condensation on walls in the summer.

Foamax provides superior insulation, comfort and cost savings, while making your walls look bright and clean!

What's That White Chalky Powder?

Efflorescence is from minerals in the concrete, mortar or soil that dissolve in water and are left behind when the water evaporates off the surface of a wall or floor. It appears as white powder or crystals and is sometimes confused with mold, but is not alive. It's not harmful, but just mineral residue that can be swept or brushed off, and a sign that water is (probably, slowly) coming through the wall or floor.

Will Mold Grow Behind ZenWall, BrightWall, CleanSpace, or Foamax Wall?

Not unless your walls are painted with latex paint or are very dirty. Mold needs organic material such as wood, paper or cardboard on which to grow. It will not grow on clean, wet concrete or plastic, unless there is dirt on the surface. In this case, the mold is growing on the dirt, not on the concrete or plastic. (Latex is rubber from trees, and therefore organic).

To keep mold from growing, we need to keep organic materials dry. In places we can't keep dry, inorganic materials such as plastic, glass, concrete, metal, etc., should be installed.

Which Is for **You**?

BEFORE

Unfinished concrete walls are cold, damp and uninviting.

All four systems drain wall leaks to a waterproofing system below, and stop water vapor from coming through the walls.

While any of the four wall systems are appropriate in dry basements, if there is ground water seepage, before or after the installation, our WaterGuard or DryTrak systems (discussed in Chapter 4) should be installed to control the water.

AFTER WITH ZENWALL

ZenWall provides that dry, clean, finished look while insulating and waterproofing your walls. This is the best-looking solution!

AFTER WITH FOAMAX

Foamax provides superior insulation, comfort and cost savings, while making your walls look bright and clean!

AFTER WITH BRIGHTWALL

BrightWall paneling brightens your basement and gives it that clean, semi-finished touch.

AFTER WITH CLEANSPACE

Covering your basement walls with the CleanSpace wall system economically brightens your basement. Use over stone walls… or as the economy version for any basement.

Basement to Beautiful Panels

Waterproof, insulated walls with integrated electrical chases and "warm" studs!

The revolutionary Basement to Beautiful panels are custom-engineered foam panels with integral studs that are fastened directly to your foundation walls. They eliminate conventional stud framing and fiberglass insulation altogether.

The panels feature a unique, advanced SilverGlo foam insulation with graphite infused throughout the foam. The graphite drives the insulation value (or R value) of the foam up by 24% over conventional foam by lowering its thermal conductivity, and gives it that silver-gray shine. At 2½ inches thick and R13, the Basement to Beautiful panels create a warm, protective blanket around your basement.

Wood studs can rot and grow mold, so there is no wood in the Basement to Beautiful panel. Instead, the panel features metal studs integrated into the foam. Metal studs, however, are highly thermally conductive and when used conventionally to frame an exterior wall in a basement against your cold foundation walls, each stud becomes a thermal bridge in the wall, creating cold spots every 16 inches and wasting energy.

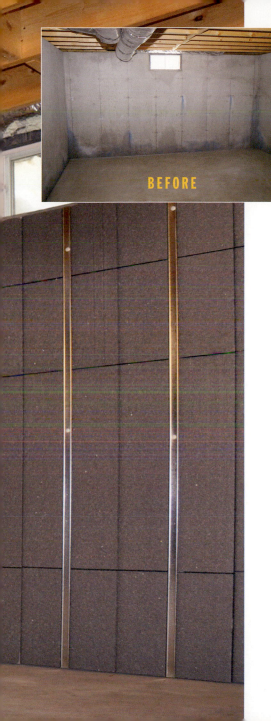

BEFORE

DURING

Walls prepared with **Basement to Beautiful™** panels.

AFTER

Completed installation of **EverLast™** panels with additional flooring, ceiling, and lighting.

EverLast™ panels are the perfect companion for Basement to Beautiful™ panels.

The Basement to Beautiful panels are not a finished wall, of course, and need to have a finished system installed over them. While there are a number of options, the best one (by far) for a basement is the Total Basement Finishing EverLast wall panel. This stylish panel is designed just for basement environments. With no drywall or paint, it won't grow mold or be damaged by water, such as plumbing leaks, which commonly flood basements and can ruin finished walls. The EverLast panels are a cement board with a washable, vinyl finish. They combine the two most popular interior colors — off white and beige — laid over a slightly alligatored texture to hide wall shine and marks. The wall is much harder than drywall and nearly impossible to dent.

You can hang anything you want on the EverLast panels, wherever you want — you don't have to find any studs. And when you want to take a nail or screw out of the wall, you can easily patch it with putty and the hole disappears into the color pattern. There's no spackling or painting — ever!

Now your walls can be warm, dry and beautiful! You can complete your basement finishing by adding electrical, ceilings and flooring — now or anytime in the future. Ask your dealer to install your Basement to Beautiful panels with the addition of the finished EverLast wall panels.

CHAPTER SEVEN

THE DOWN LOW
Suitable Basement Flooring

Imagine walking around your basement barefoot. No dust or dampness or freezing cold assaulting your soles as you shuffle from the laundry area to the storage closet — or from the TV to the sofa. And no worries that next week or next month or next year the whole thing will have to be torn out due to water damage.

This is not an unattainable dream. Let me show you your choices...

To most people who have had a series of unsettling wet basement episodes, the idea of laying a carpet and using that part of the house as finished space is one that would never seem possible. But think about it now. So far we have prevented the whole basement floor from getting wet with a WaterGuard system around the full perimeter of the basement and we have kept it that way with a TripleSafe sump pump system. Then we made the walls nice and dry with one of the wall systems. So now we don't have a wet basement floor — we have a damp one instead.

Damp floor! Now hold the phone! you say. What do you mean damp?

Well, we have controlled the groundwater leakage, but there is another much slower way moisture can move into our space. Water vapor can pass through the floor slab, because concrete is porous and the ground is damp. In newer homes built by good builders who care, there may be a plastic vapor barrier under the floor, installed before the floor was poured.

This means, you probably don't have one. In fact, we almost never encounter a vapor barrier under a floor when installing sump pump systems.

Water vapor passing through a slab is a slow process. As moisture passes through, it evaporates off the surface of the basement floor, so the floor doesn't appear wet. However, if we install a carpet on top of the slab, the carpeting slows the evaporation process down, and the moisture builds up in the carpeting.

The high relative humidity in the carpeting causes mold to grow, which causes that musty smell that makes basement spaces so unpleasant. Besides that, it can rot the carpet, requiring premature replacement. And anyone allergic to mold is not going to be a happy camper in the basement.

For us earth dwellers, the floor is the surface of a room that we are in constant contact with. Carpet laid over hard, cold, damp concrete doesn't feel as comfortable as carpet on a softer, warmer, and completely dry subfloor.

So what can you do?

The old-fashioned "I had no other choice" option is to lay a wood floor down and put carpet on that. This sounds good — until the wood floor starts to rot and smell. And who has 3 or 4 inches of headroom to lose in a basement?

The biggest problem with wood subfloors, or any floor in a basement that involves wood, is that one day you will have to replace the floor when it gets wet from a plumbing leak. (I am assuming you have opted to go with the TripleSafe sump pump system. If not, add pump failure to plumbing leaks as the tragic events that WILL happen and make your life miserable for a month or so, and leave you poorer.)

Your basement is a big hole under a structure you call your home. Your home is full of pipes. Drain pipes and pressurized supply pipes. You also have tubs, toilets, showers, dishwashers, a refrigerator with a water line to it for ice and water, and sinks. If (I should say "when") something goes wrong, and water leaks, overflows, bursts, or otherwise escapes out of this plumbing system, where do you think it will wind up?

*(**Hint:** Remember Janesky's First Law of Hydrodynamics — water flows downhill.)*

Right, in the basement. So now you have a wooden subfloor, invariably made of plywood or chipboard, that is soaked through, top and bottom, and the carpet, like a wet sponge, lying on it. Typically, this subfloor remains wet for a long time because you can't get the water out from under the subfloor. Unless... You guessed it.

You rip up the carpet and rip up the wood subfloor and start over. Hopefully the stud walls are not built on top of the wood subfloor, or you'll also have to... oh... trust me.

Important!

No Wood Subfloors In Basements!

I know. The suspense is killing you.

There is only one solution. A subfloor made entirely of products that are unaffected by water, water vapor and mold. One word: plastic. ThermalDry Floor systems are the only plastic, all-inorganic subfloors in the world. Water won't ruin them. Water vapor won't go through them. Mold won't grow on them.

Traditional carpets and wood floors are not appropriate for a basement and will not last. ThermalDry Basement Floor systems are the answer. ThermalDry Floor systems are designed just for basements.

A ThermalDry floor is made up of 12-inch square modular tiles with a carpeted or tiled finish on top. They have raised pegs on the bottom of them to suspend your basement floor above the cold, hard, damp concrete floor, allowing your floor to breathe. Water vapor does not get trapped in the finished flooring, and if there is a leak, the water can be dried from under the floor without removing and destroying the ThermalDry tiles.

VARIETY IN YOUR BASEMENT FLOOR? You bet! ThermalDry's modular design allows a custom architectural look by mixing carpet and tiles.

A PLACE FOR WATER The bottom of ThermalDry Flooring has pegs to create an air space under your floor. This keeps water vapor from getting trapped underneath your finished floor — causing odors and mold.

MOCHA

CHARCOAL

SANDSTONE

CANYON BEIGE

PARQUET

UNFINISHED

An advantage of ThermalDry's modular design is that tile and carpet can be mixed and matched to achieve a custom architectural look. And in the future, if one spot in your floor gets damaged or worn — a high-traffic area at the bottom of the stairs, for example — you can switch the damaged tiles with undamaged ones from an area that never gets seen, like a closet or a hidden corner. Or you can use new tiles to replace just the worn ones — something you can't do with any other flooring. If the basement gets wet temporarily, it is not likely you will have to replace anything — just dry it out quickly.

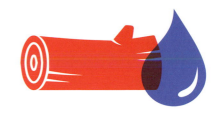

Wood + Water = Bad

Subfloor tiles available at big box stores made of chipboard with dimpled plastic material on the bottom are a disaster waiting to happen. Not only does the wood floor get wet, but the plastic dimples beneath are facing up and fill with water in the event of a plumbing leak, sealing your floor's doom.

Repeat after me: Wood plus water equals BAD! Forget the wood on a basement floor.

MOCHA CARPET TILES

CANYON BEIGE TILES

PARQUET TILES

UNFINISHED THERMALDRY FLOOR MATTING READY FOR YOUR CARPETING

ThermalDry Parquet Flooring

If you want the warm look of wood in your basement, we have just what you need! Real wood should never be installed on a basement floor because it absorbs water vapor from the concrete slab and swells, gets moldy and rots. And just one plumbing leak will ruin your wood floor in hours.

Our popular ThermalDry parquet flooring has no wood at all and will not be affected by moisture or water in any way. It has all the benefits of modular ThermalDry flooring along with the wood look you want!

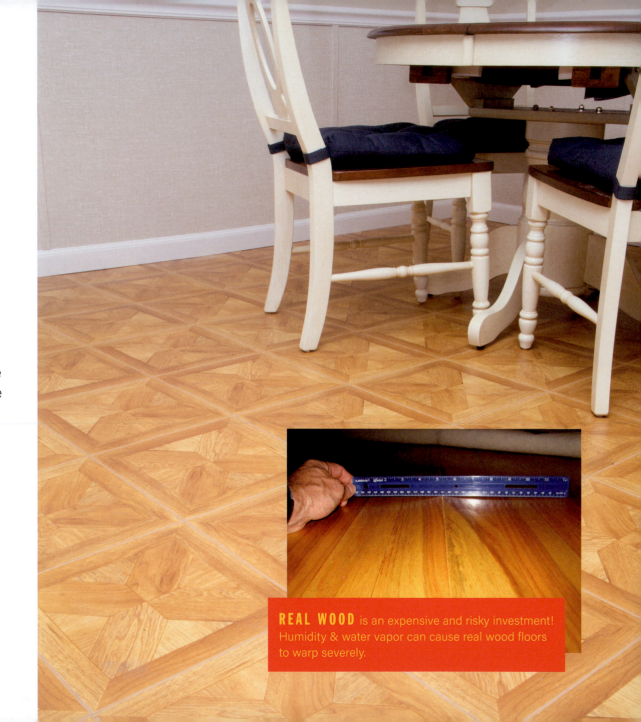

REAL WOOD is an expensive and risky investment! Humidity & water vapor can cause real wood floors to warp severely.

ThermalDry Floor Matting

If you want a different color carpeting than charcoal or mocha, but still want the benefits of ThermalDry flooring, we have just what you need! Our unfinished ThermalDry Floor matting panels provide an air space under the floor and a thermal break from the cold slab, creating a subfloor that will not rot, grow mold or get damaged from a leak.

DRY CARPETS. ThermalDry provides an air space under your carpet so water vapor doesn't get trapped and fester into odors and mold.

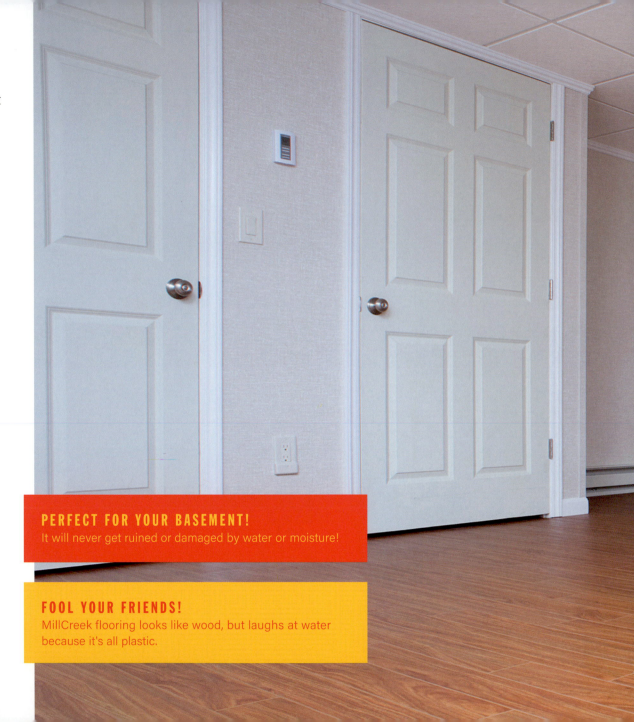

You love the look of wood floors... but your basement floor is likely to get wet from water vapor, a plumbing leak, or a surprise leak from a big rain — which would surely ruin a wood floor. What can you do?

MillCreek waterproof flooring is the answer!

MillCreek uses a patented process that produces the textured grain of hardwood out of PVC, giving MillCreek flooring the same look, feel and touch as a hardwood floor — without the wood! And when your basement gets wet, you don't have to worry about your floor being ruined. Tests have proven it can be used in any environment, with no influence from humidity.

A MillCreek floor looks great and is resistant to water — but if you have a basement where a lot of roughhousing is going on, I'd stick with the ThermalDry tiles. MillCreek flooring is not modular, and replacing a plank that gets damaged is not so easy.

PERFECT FOR YOUR BASEMENT!
It will never get ruined or damaged by water or moisture!

FOOL YOUR FRIENDS!
MillCreek flooring looks like wood, but laughs at water because it's all plastic.

Finishing your basement?

Contact the experts at:
www.TotalBasementFinishing.com
to find your local dealer.

HOME GYM   **FAMILY ROOM**   **GAME ROOM**

TBF Total
BASEMENT
Finishing
From Basement to Beautiful!™

CHAPTER EIGHT

THE AIR DOWN THERE
Mastering Humidity

Mold. It's one of a homeowner's chief fears. Mold damages property, causes illness, makes a basement smell like a basement, and too often makes the whole house smell like the basement. It can be controlled by one simple principle: Remove moisture from the air. When the air is dry, your stuff is dry, and when your stuff is dry mold doesn't stand a chance. Here's how to do it.

There are four ways basements become wet or damp:

1. Groundwater leakage.
(We have this one taken care of in the chapters we've covered so far).

2. Capillary action.
It means wicking. For example, a block wall may not leak, but it feels damp because it's wicking the water inside it to the surface like a sponge.

3. Water vapor coming through your walls and floor.
(By installing one of the wall systems and our ThermalDry Floor matting, we don't have to worry about wicking because we've slowed water vapor transmission considerably.)

4. Exterior air leaking into your basement.
This is not a problem as long as the outside air is cooler than the basement. It's the warmer summertime air that moves lots of moisture into our basement.

Whenever the outside air is warmer than the inside air, and especially when it's humid outside air, we are likely to have a condensation problem in our subterranean spaces. This is because the relative humidity of air goes up 2.2% for each 1°F you cool it. Our basements are always cool because they are below ground. And we know that a house is like a chimney — air flows upward and escapes through the upper levels, with new air being sucked in at the lower levels.

So when it's hot and humid in the summer, rain or no rain, our basement may be the wettest it has been all year!

High Humidity

If it's an 80°F day with relative humidity of 80%, and we suck this air into our basements and cool it to 68°F, the relative humidity goes up by 26.4% (12°F x 2.2%). But wait a minute, 80% plus 26.4% is more than 100%, and we can't have more than 100%. So instead, as the air becomes saturated, it gives up its moisture onto your cold basement walls, floor, water tank, and pipes. This is called condensation.

Even without condensation, we still get high relative humidity levels, which allows mold to grow and cause "stinky basement syndrome." And dust mites are having a party. More on that later.

In order to eliminate condensation, you need either to heat the basement (ridiculous in summer) or take water out of it (easy to do). Correction: I should say take water out of it efficiently and effectively (not so easy unless you have the right equipment).

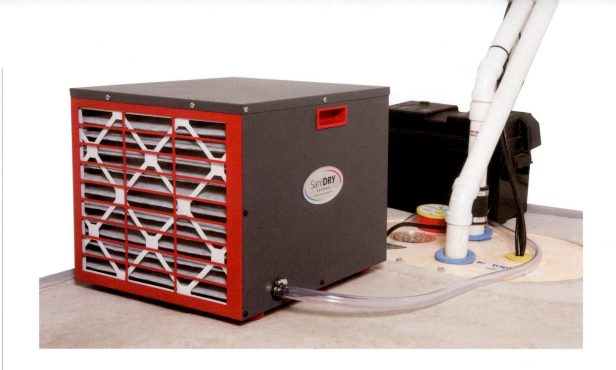

Not Just Any Dehumidifier

A dehumidifier is the answer. But not just any dehumidifier. I have been dealing with this issue intensely for nearly 30 years. The only machine that will get you the results you need is called the **SaniDry Sedona**. It's awesome.

The SaniDry Sedona is a high-capacity, high-efficiency dehumidification system, with air filtration, in a single unit. The SaniDry Sedona removes 100 pints of water per day out of your basement air, while using the same energy as a "40 pint" dehumidifier. And it filters particles out of the air to less than an incredible two microns in size — which is smaller than any mold spore or dust mite dropping.

The SaniDry Sedona basement air system wrings your air dry, and its powerful blower moves that dry air out into and around your basement space. This dry air then dries your building materials and basement contents, which makes the damp smell and damp feeling go away! What a huge difference a SaniDry Sedona can make in "condensation season." People really love their dry basement environments after having a SaniDry Sedona installed.

You'll also never have to empty any buckets with your SaniDry Sedona because it automatically drains into your WaterGuard system or sump.

Having a groundwater-free basement is one thing. Adding a SaniDry Sedona is like placing the cherry on top of your dry basement program. It makes it complete.

All below-grade spaces need one. Picture the concrete in your basement turning white because it is so dry!

The SaniDry Sedona is Energy Star rated — a rare achievement for a dehumidification system. Not only that, it is the most efficient dehumidifier in the world!*

Another big benefit of the SaniDry Sedona air system is that it doesn't have to be in the space it's drying. You can locate it in a utility room and duct the wet air in and dry air out to the main room of your basement.

With no water leaks and dry air, materials stay dry and you can finish your basement or use it for storage. No smell, no mold, no property damage.

*Without a bulky heat exchange core which doubles its size and makes a lot of noise.

How does it perform so incredibly well with the same amount of energy that less-effective 20-pound-weakling dehumidifiers use?

1. Designed to perform in lower air temperatures found in basements and crawl spaces.

2. Larger, higher performace components (compressor, condenser and evaporator coils).

3. Processes (filters and dries) 300 cubic feet of your basement air per minute compared to about 50 cfm for other models.

POWERFUL BLOWER. The blower really moves dehumidified air around to dry the entire space.

Did I mention I love the SaniDry Sedona? I know you will, too.

Why Household Dehumidifiers Just Don't Do the Job

1. The unit is too small.

2. The cold coil (the actual thing that takes the water out of the air) **is too small.**

3. **The fan is too small.** (It has to be so it doesn't blow the air past the dinky coil too fast, otherwise it wouldn't take any water out!)

4. The fan doesn't circulate the dry air around your basement — because it's too small.

5. They usually aren't drained automatically, so the bucket fills up and they shut off.

6. They are rated to remove only 25 pints, 30 pints, 40 pints, etc. per day at 80°F air temperature. Warm air holds a lot more moisture than cold air. Put them in a 68°F basement and their effectiveness goes way down below this number.

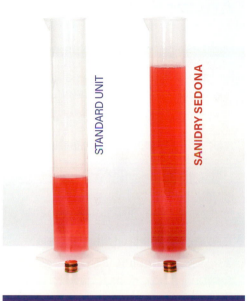

STANDARD UNIT

SANIDRY SEDONA

Water (colored for visibility) removed by standard household dehumidifier vs. SaniDry Sedona **for same electricity cost.**

There is simply no comparison between a SaniDry Sedona and any dehumidifier you've ever seen. I am usually a bit conservative and always realistic about what a product can do. The SaniDry Sedona is one product where I let all the performance promises hang out.

Open Sump Hole?

Having an open sump hole and running a dehumidifier is like trying to fill a bucket with a hole in it. As you dry the air, more water evaporates into it via the open sump hole with a pool of water sitting in it all year. In other words, you have a dehumidifier and a humidifier.

Dehumidifiers Should Drain Automatically

Quick: How many hours in a week? **168.**

How long would it take a cheapo dehumidifier's bucket to fill up and shut off? **Maybe 12.**

If you empty it once a week, what percentage of the time is it actually running? **If you're not a mathlete, the answer is 7% of the time. Meaning it's off 93% of the time.**

Who wants to have "Empty dehumidifier bucket" on their daily chore sheet? The answer is to **hook it up with a hose to drain the water away automatically** — and you never have to empty it.

Question: What Makes a Basement Smell Like One?
Answer: Mold

Mold can grow in a waterproofed basement.

Mold needs organic material to grow (which you have), and high relative humidity — over 60% to 70%. It doesn't have to be wet for mold to grow, just humid. In fact, mold won't grow underwater.

A SaniDry Sedona ensures that the relative humidity stays below 55% all year long.

There are a lot of mold experts. One who tells you to eliminate the mold without eliminating the water and humidity is not helping you. Some tell you to coat your floor joists and other structural elements with anti-mold paint.

This implies that if it's humid and mold wants to grow, the paint will stop it from growing. Assuming that's true, what about the contents of your basement? If you have a cardboard box, does it have to be painted, too? How about your sofa? Call me crazy, but if it's really dry down there with low humidity, mold won't grow with or without a coating.

(I'm not crazy; that's the way it works.)

Dry, Clean Air – The Ultimate Purifier

Air is a very small thing. It gets in, around and between all your contents and building materials — into the smallest places. If that air has been dried by a SaniDry Sedona, it picks up moisture from these contents (dries them) and goes through the Sedona to be dried again — and out to the space to dry your contents once more. Dry air dries things, and mold doesn't stand a chance on dry things.

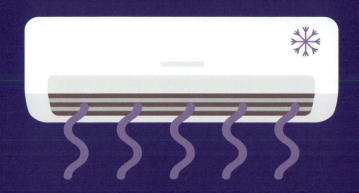

Save Money
Dry Air is Easier to Cool!

Damp indoor air costs more money to cool. Sure, there's a small cost to running a SaniDry Sedona, but lower cooling costs partly offset this electricity cost. This is because your central air system has to remove the moisture from the air in order to cool it, and that takes energy. Air conditioning systems are inefficient at dehumidifying.

If you dry the air in your basement, that air rises into the rest of the house, making the whole house drier. You'll also feel more comfortable at a higher temperature with less humidity in the whole house.

SaniDry Sedona – Energy Test Winner!

We tested four dehumidifiers to find out the cost per pint of water removed from the air. The worst performer was a standard household unit available under any number of recognizable brand names. It came out at more than 11 cents per pint removed. A higher priced unit, but without the features of the SaniDry Sedona, cost about 10 cents per pint of water removed. The big winner was the SaniDry Sedona, which cost only 3.3 cents per pint of water removed! What a bargain!

Dust Mites
#1 INDOOR ALLERGEN

Continued from Chapter 1.

The No. 1 thing that people with asthma and allergies react to indoors is dust mite droppings. Dust mites live in your furniture, bedding, and carpeting and feed off dead skin flakes. Their droppings are so small that they become airborne, are breathed in and thus can irritate humans. Dust mites need relative humidity above 50% to live, as they absorb water out of the air rather than drinking it. Therefore, dry the air and dust mites die.

We have heard of a doctor in West Virginia who prescribed a SaniDry unit on his prescription pad! Now there's an enlightened doctor!

For more information go to **www. housedustmite.org.**

The idea, they say, is that wet air is heavier than dry air, so if you suck air out of your house from near the basement floor, you are exhausting the wettest air. The problem is that it's not true. Warm air holds a lot more water than cold air, and everyone knows that warm air rises. The reason there is more humidity in the basement, as previously noted, is that the basement is cold, and when air is cooled the relative humidity goes up unless we remove water from the air.

The problem with exhausting air out of your house is that it is "conditioned" air — you paid to cool or heat it, and in the process dehumidify it, via your HVAC system. If you exhaust this air out, then new air has to come in to replace it. Where does the new air come from? Outside, of course. And unless it's a perfect day outside, like 70°F and 50% relative humidity, outside air needs to be heated or cooled and dehumidified to be comfortable, and that costs money.

Fan-in-a-Box
Too Good to Be True

Some waterproofing contractors offer another unit that debuted on the market around 2003. In truth, most of these contractors do not even understand why the unit is a bad idea, and just go by the manufacturer's recommendations. The unit consists of a fan in a tall sheet metal cabinet with a humidistat on it and an exhaust duct to the outside, like a dryer vent. The way it's supposed to work is when the humidity gets high the fan automatically turns on, sucks air off the basement floor and exhausts it outside. New air is supposed to come down from upstairs, where it's drier, and this air is supposed to dry your basement.

The brochures on these fan-in-a-box units explain that they only cost pennies in electricity to run. That's true. But it costs a lot more than that in air conditioning and heating bills, which you are probably not going to associate with this unit. Everyone is aware of energy saving things to do like caulking, weather stripping, insulating, and installing tighter windows and doors. Why would you put a fan to blow air out of (and suck air into) your home on purpose? There are other issues regarding ventilation, but most homes are so leaky... well, that's another book.

You've already invested money in your indoor air, so stick with it and dehumidify it.

Keep Basement Windows Closed!

There is no reason to open a basement window for any type of climate control. When the air outside is cooler than inside, you lose heat. When it's warmer outside, you bring in moisture. Keep basement windows closed.

In fact, replacing basement windows with double panes of energy-efficient glass that are fixed — and don't open — is the most energy-efficient option.

! *Skip this section if you don't have any basement windows.*

CHAPTER NINE

SEEING DAYLIGHT
Getting the Windows Right

Light is at a premium in the basement. Most of us are not going for the dark and gloomy look, so any daylight you can bring in is a prized commodity. Just make sure you're not letting in water or humidity along with the added brightness. When you think about waterproofing your basement and fixing it up, you should think about your basement windows.

THERE ARE THREE ISSUES.

1. Do the windows leak water?
   If so, we need to install drains.

2. Are the windows rusted, rotted, drafty, or ugly?
   If so, replace them.

3. Are the window wells ugly, rusty, and open?
   If so, replace them.

IF YOUR BASEMENT WINDOWS LEAK WHEN IT RAINS HARD, IT'S PROBABLY BECAUSE OF ONE OF THE FOLLOWING THREE REASONS.

1. The gutters are overflowing into the window wells.

2. The ground around the window is pitched toward the house.

3. A downspout is dumping lots of water near the window.

They Aren't Submarine Windows

When there is water outside of a basement window, it will leak into the basement. After all, they aren't submarine windows! So we need to fix them.

Besides the obvious — fix the gutters, re-grade if possible, and extend the downspouts — if you don't do something else, the window will likely leak again in the future. The best thing to do is install a drain from the window well to the perimeter drainage system around your basement that leads to the sump pump.

In the event that water rises in the window well, a simple system called WellDuct, a vertical extension of the WaterGuard system, drains water from the well before the window leaks.

A drain hole is drilled through your basement wall just under the windowsill. If the wall is a block wall, the hole is lined with a section of pipe. Then a grate is installed on the outside over the hole.

The WellDuct conduit itself is installed on the inside of your basement wall.

If water rises to threaten the window, it goes through the grate, through the wall, down the WellDuct, through your inside drain system, and to the sump pump. Simple.

It's a good idea to cover the grate with clean stone outside to keep leaves from plugging it — unless you have a SunHouse (keep reading).

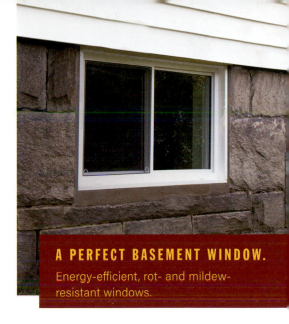

A PERFECT BASEMENT WINDOW.
Energy-efficient, rot- and mildew-resistant windows.

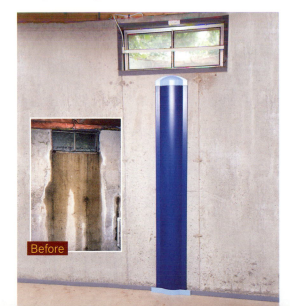

Before

Everlasting Windows

If your windows look bad or are rotted or drafty, replace them.

Now is the time to do this. New EverLast energy-efficient, all-vinyl windows can be installed to replace your old ones. The new windows look much better, don't let wind in, have double-pane glass, and never need paint — perfect for the damp environment close to the ground.

What Are You Looking At?

If your window wells are rusty, ugly, or open at the top, they can be dramatically improved. Window wells without covers let in leaves and debris, and rain and gutter overflow water gets in. The dirt bottom allows weeds to grow and mud to splash up onto your windows. All this makes for a pretty lousy view from inside the basement — the space you want to improve.

The Answer Is a Great Product Called SunHouse Basement Window Enclosures

The light-colored SunHouse window well features a sturdy, clear cover that fits nicely and a bottom that prevents weed growth and keeps leaves, debris, and rain out. One of the SunHouse's best benefits is that with the clean, light-colored bottom a lot more sunlight bounces into your basement and brightens up a space where we can use all the light we can get.

LOOKS GREAT!
The SunHouse basement window enclosure really dresses up what used to be an eyesore. Bright and clean.

"Carpenter Ready"

If you plan to finish your basement at any time in the future, now is the time to address the basement windows, walls, floors and air and make your basement "carpenter ready." Carpenters don't know a lot about basement windows, and nothing about window wells or the drainage of them. It's just not their thing. Have a waterproofing contractor who deals with these products every day take care of it for you.

Basement Bedroom Code

If you are making bedrooms in your basement, you need to check the local codes about "egress" window requirements. Basically, in case of a fire you need two ways out of a bedroom. The door is one, and a window big enough to climb out of to the surface can be another.

Keep Windows Closed!

Even though EverLast basement windows are smooth-operating windows and easy to open, I can think of no reason to ever open a window in a basement other than to pass a long object through, such as a ladder. In cooler weather we want to keep cold air out. In warm weather we want to keep warm air out to avoid condensation problems.

OLD

NEW

The SunHouse will reflect a lot more light into your basement!

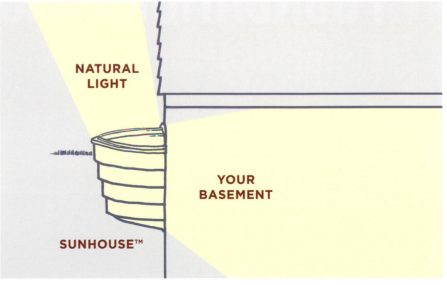

NATURAL LIGHT

YOUR BASEMENT

SUNHOUSE™

! *Skip this section if you have block walls, stone walls, or if you have a poured foundation without leaking wall cracks.*

CHAPTER TEN

FOUNDATION FRACTURES
Fixing Wall Cracks

· ·

Let's say you are willing to live with your basement walls as they are, except for a few leaky cracks. You're not eager to install any kind of covering or panels. At the same time, you'd like to be sure your house isn't about to fall down. Here's what to do...

Concrete Cracks

There are two things a concrete man will tell you he can guarantee about his product: **It will get hard and it will crack.**

Cracks in poured concrete walls are common. Most are a result of shrinkage of the concrete as part of the curing process. Often the cracks will be in the middle third of the wall, or from the corner of a window, which is a weak spot in the wall. Most wall cracks pose no structural concern. If you live in a new house, don't bother calling your lawyer — your builder is not a monster. The most common problem wall cracks cause is water leaking through them.

You can fix them by digging it up and patching it outside. But that's a big hole, and it's messy. Whatever you patch the cracks with can fail and if it leaks again, what are you going to do — dig it up all over again? Also, there may be something in the way outside that prevents you from digging a big hole there — such as a driveway, sidewalk, deck, or porch.

Many methods have been developed over the years to fix wall cracks from the inside. Whenever you hear that "many methods have been developed over the years" to do anything, you have to conclude that people were not satisfied with the previous methods. This is true for crack repair.

Patching Rarely Works

The first thing not to do is try to patch a crack on the surface of the wall inside. Even if you chisel out the crack a bit before you jam in any miracle compound, your chances of success are slim. Why? Because wall cracks move. Changes in the soil's moisture level can cause the wall to swell or shrink, hot and cold seasonal changes make the wall move, and the earth outside uses the crack as an expansion and contraction joint. So the miracle goo either splits in the middle or loses its bond with the concrete and then the wall leaks again.

Another older, fairly popular method that's still used in some areas is to inject epoxy into the crack. Think of it as crazy glue: usually clear, goes in as a liquid, sticks well, and dries rock hard. The problem is that epoxy allows no flexibility for movement. When the wall wants to move, the epoxy can't, so it either breaks loose or a new crack develops. To improve on this, someone invented a urethane liquid that could be injected into the crack and dry like a rubbery material. The logic is that this material is flexible so it can move with wall. Sounds good in theory. The problem is that a crack that is only 1/16 inch can easily open to 1/8 inch—which is 100% bigger. Unfortunately, urethane won't stretch that far. Not even close.

A COMMON SIGHT.
A crack that has been repaired many times is still leaking.

Another problem with injecting stuff into a crack is that if there is dirt in a crack that washed in with the water, the dirt prevents the stuff you inject from getting a good bond to the sides of the crack.

Let me be realistic. All of the above methods for fixing a wall crack can work. But their track record shows they don't work all the time. And the more years that go by following the repair, the higher the probability that these repairs will leak again.

Going on our premise that we only want to do things once, and that we want our basement dry all the time, we need to find a better way. It just so happens I know one. In fact, like a lot of the things you read in this book, *I developed and patented it.*

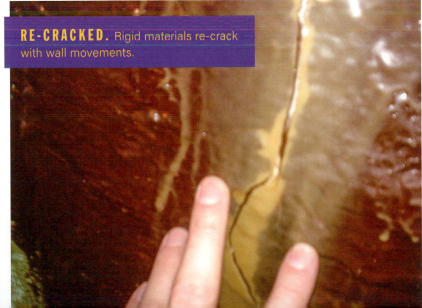

RE-CRACKED. Rigid materials re-crack with wall movements.

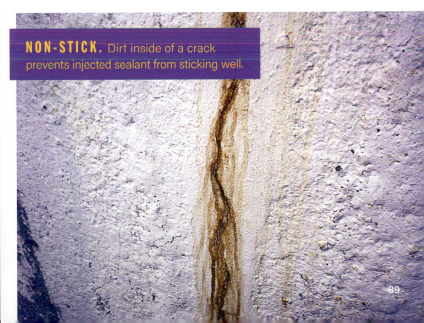

NON-STICK. Dirt inside of a crack prevents injected sealant from sticking well.

FlexiSpan Crack Repair Works Every Time

FlexiSpan seals the crack and provides a built-in secondary repair strategy in case the seal fails. First, a small drywell is developed into the floor under the crack. If we can connect into the perimeter drainage system or a stone bed under the floor, great. If not, we make our own drywell about 5 to 10 gallons in size. Then we seal the crack with a urethane-based sealant (not the same urethane that we talked about being injected on the previous page). Next a special polyurethane ether foam strip is applied over the first seal. This foam strip is set up so water from within and behind it can drain into the drywell. Then it is overlaid with polyurethane sealant and tooled off to look like a gray drywall compound joint. Lastly, the opening in the floor is re-concreted.

Now your wall crack is sealed, and if any water ever gets past the seal, it drains down into the drywell. The results you are looking for, a dry wall and dry floor, are achieved — forever — because FlexiSpan is... well, flexible. Very flexible, and no amount of wall movement will make it leak again.

FLEXIBLE. FlexiSpan gets results — a dry wall and a dry floor.

FlexiSpan is a great innovation that works like a charm. It's especially appreciated in the Midwest where the wall movement can be very substantial. In some cases, a crack may be injected with something and a FlexiSpan repair will be installed over it anyway to ensure there will be no problems in the future. This may be done on a really bad leaker, or a very large crack.

A BETTER SOLUTION.
With multiple wall cracks, install BrightWall paneling to drain leaks into a perimeter WaterGuard system.

Lots of Cracks?
Opt for Full Protection

If you have lots of wall cracks, you may just consider installing a WaterGuard system and BrightWall paneling over your leaking wall cracks without doing anything else to them. This way, you get a dry floor and dry walls, and if you discover floor/wall joint leakage in the future, you aren't starting from scratch to fix that problem. If you spent money to fix five wall cracks, for example, you only have a warranty on those five wall cracks, not on the floor or any other wall imperfections.

When Cracks are More than Cracks

If your cracks are very large, or if you run your finger across a foundation crack and it's uneven (one side higher than the other), you should get advice from a foundation structural repair contractor. Big cracks indicate wall buckling or vertical movement in your foundation, usually caused by clay soils swelling and shrinking. Your waterproofing contractor may be a structural repair contractor as well. You can find a contractor who specializes in structural repair at www.foundationsupportworks.com.

Leaking Pipe Penetrations

Leaking pipe penetrations can be dealt with in the same way as wall cracks. Pipes can have lots of movement in and out of the wall as they expand and contract along their length. All the same older methods have been done with pipes as with wall cracks. FlexiSpan can be used on a pipe penetration for a reliable, effective cure.

! *Skip this section if you don't have a crawl space.*

CHAPTER ELEVEN

CRAWL SPACE HELL
Causes and Solutions

The name says it all. You have to stoop over, or maybe even literally crawl, to enter it. And you know all too well that you're not the only creature crawling in there. It's home to bugs and dirt and a damp, unpleasant smell.

You would only go in there when it's unavoidable. You don't even like to think about it. You're pretty sure it's bad for your home to sit above all that open dirt (mud, mold, dust). Maybe it's time to transform it...

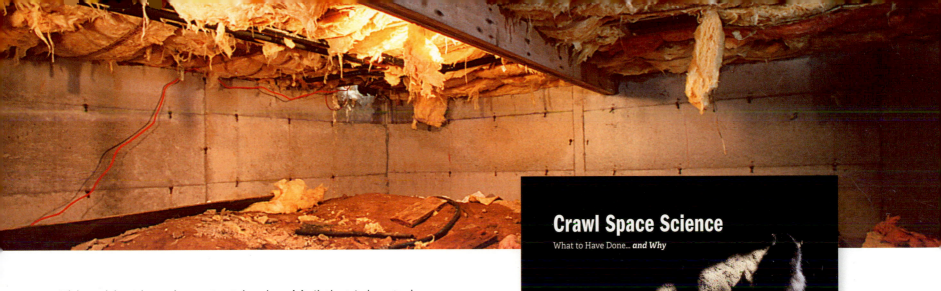

This subject is so important (and so **big**!) that I devoted a whole book to it called Crawl Space Science. If you have a crawl space, you should get this book from your local Basement Systems dealer or CleanSpace installer.

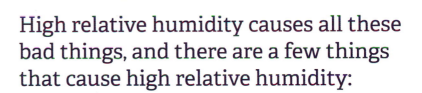

There is only one cause of all the problems in crawl spaces — relative humidity. When it's high it can ...

- Cause mold to grow
- Cause your floor to rot
- Make a haven for insects of all sorts
- Cause odors
- Waste energy by increasing heating and cooling costs
- Cause all the above effects upstairs and throughout the house
- And these things affect your property value.
  Who wants to buy a house with a problem?

High relative humidity causes all these bad things, and there are a few things that cause high relative humidity:

- Leaking groundwater through your crawl space walls that lies there and soaks the soil
- Exposed earth on the floor of the crawl space
- Open vents to the outside

So What Do We Do?

For the groundwater, we install a sump pump system (same considerations as Chapter 5, but we typically use the SmartSump system, specially designed for crawl spaces) and make sure the water leaking in gets to it instead of ponding. For the wet walls and exposed earth, we install the patented CleanSpace crawl space encapsulation system, and for the open vents, we close them — permanently — with CleanSpace vent covers.

A "Smart" Crawl Space Sump Pump System

Part of keeping your crawl space dry involves a sump pump — but not just any sump pump installation will do. Basement Systems' SmartSump is designed just for crawl spaces.

The SmartSump has a high-quality, ⅓ hp Zoeller cast iron pump, with automatic float switch. The lid and unique sump liner are designed to accept the CleanSpace system, for an airtight seal. The SmartSump has a unique lid design, so water from a plumbing leak fills an alarm pocket on the lid first, sounding a WaterWatch alarm that will let you know there is a plumbing leak. From there, the water flows down a special airtight floor drain that will let the water down, but will not let damp air up into your crawl space. The WaterWatch alarm also alerts you to pump failure for any reason, including power outages.

SmartSump is a smart idea for your crawl space!

Seal All Air Leaks to the Outside

When a CleanSpace system is installed, you want to seal vents to keep out evil unconditioned outside air. But vents aren't the only way outside air can get into your crawl space. Spaces under the sill plate and around pipes and wires to the outside, poorly fitting or rotted hatch doors, and other odd openings are all paths that need to be sealed to get the best results.

One area that was previously ignored is the open cavities in the top of block walls. Block walls are most common in dirt crawl spaces. Outside air goes right through porous block walls and up out of the top of the wall into the inside of the crawl space. To seal the top of the block walls, a product called CleanSpace Wall Cap works great. It's an L-shaped molding that slips right on top of the block wall, covering the space the sill plate does not. The clear plastic allows for termite inspections without removing it.

The CleanSpace crawl space encapsulation system is a heavy duty 7-layer liner material, like a pool liner. It gets installed across the floor and up the walls and sealed around all piers and pipes, etc. It stops all the water vapor from the walls or soil and is very durable, so you can't poke holes in it, rip it, or pull it down off the walls when you crawl in there. And yes, you'll have no problem crawling into your crawl space once the CleanSpace liner is installed — it's that clean, bright white, and nice! It has an antimicrobial ingredient molded into the material to resist mold and bacteria growth. It will also last as long as the house. Besides that, it looks fantastic. Talk about a crawl space makeover!

HEAVEN AND HELL. A CleanSpace system turns crawl space hell into crawl space heaven.

What About the Vents?

Vents are sealed with vent covers installed outside. The building code required these vents when your home was built. The building code was wrong and made your problem worse by letting in hot, humid air in the summer, which caused condensation and rot and mold. In the winter these vents let in freezing cold air, making your floors upstairs cold and wasting energy. The building codes are now changing, and in the future vented dirt crawl spaces will be a thing of the past.

BEFORE

AFTER The CleanSpace vent covers seal the air out, insulate, and improve the appearance.

Your Crawl Space Access Door Should Seal Tight

Many crawl spaces have an access door to the outside. Most often it is made of plywood, and because it's down by the ground it rots easily. These rotted, warped doors usually seal poorly and look like heck. The answer is an all-plastic door that won't rot, warp, or need paint and that bugs won't eat. Perfect.

Knobs screw into anchors in the wall to draw the door tight against weather stripping to seal off outside air.

A snug-fitting all-plastic door stops air and moisture from entering.

Fixing Your Crawl Space Pays for Itself

A vented dirt crawl space is a huge energy waster. The outside air constantly flowing into your home increases the heat and air conditioning load. And the dampness needs to be wrung out of the air by your air conditioning system, which puts a heavy tax on it — and you. It costs you real dollars in energy bills, not to mention the cost of wood replacement, mold cleanup, and property-value reduction.

An independent study revealed that homeowners who properly fix their vented dirt crawl space can save 10% to 20% on their heating and air conditioning costs! In my opinion, if the conditions are right (meaning all wrong before the installation), you can save more than that. CleanSpace is one of those things that you are going to pay for whether you get it or not. That makes it a no-brainer to get.

When we developed the CleanSpace system in 1999, heating oil was $1.69 a gallon and natural gas was $2.50 per Mcf (thousand cubic feet). In the years since then, prices have risen by as much as 200% (or more) and then come back down, but they have never been lower. This means that fixing your vented dirt crawl space is low-hanging fruit in your "green choices garden." It pays for itself quickly and is a good financial investment.

Crawl Space Insulation

Insulation should be installed between heated and unheated spaces. In your crawl space that place is the walls. Once the vents have been closed up.

A great way to insulate your crawl space walls is with SilverGlo foam boards. The foam is infused with graphite particles, which bump up the insulation value 24% over regular foam. It also has a radiant barrier (foil face) to reflect heat back into your house.

Besides eliminating heat loss in the winter, SilverGlo reduces the risk of condensation on the walls in hot summer months.

NOT LIKE THE OTHERS. SilverGlo insulation panels look different because they are different — infused graphite particles bump up the insulation value by 24% over regular foam.

Dehumidifying Your Crawl Space

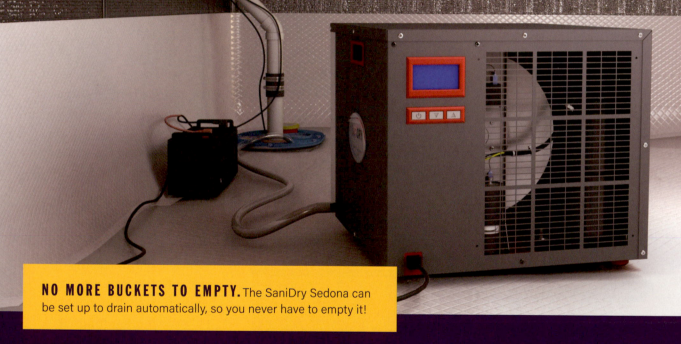

NO MORE BUCKETS TO EMPTY. The SaniDry Sedona can be set up to drain automatically, so you never have to empty it!

Once a sump system and a CleanSpace liner are installed, and the vents are closed, the "cherry on top" is a dehumidification system. In Chapter 8, we described the SaniDry Sedona, the world's most efficient, high-performance dehumidifier and filtration system*. This system fits easily in crawl spaces.

Remember, you are not just dehumidifying the crawl space (or basement). Because air rises from the bottom to the top of your home, the air that now rises will dry your house instead of wetting it.

*Without a bulky heat exchange core which doubles its size and makes a lot of noise.

Provide for Plumbing Leaks in Your Crawl Space

In a dirt crawl space a plumbing leak will drain into the dirt forever (because you'll never notice it), keeping the dirt wet and the humidity up. When a CleanSpace system is installed, a plumbing leak can fill up your crawl space like a swimming pool. The sump systems described in Chapter 5, SuperSump and TripleSafe, have airtight lids with airtight floor drains that drain water from the top of the CleanSpace liner in the event of a plumbing leak in your crawl space.

If you don't have groundwater leakage you won't need a sump system in your crawl space with your CleanSpace system. However, you still need to provide for plumbing leaks. You can do this with a SmartDrain.

A SmartDrain is a drywell-type unit that can be installed in your crawl space along with the CleanSpace liner. It features an alarm and an airtight floor drain in its lid. In the event of a plumbing leak, the alarm sounds, alerting you to the leak, and the water drains away into the soil under the CleanSpace until you get the leak fixed.

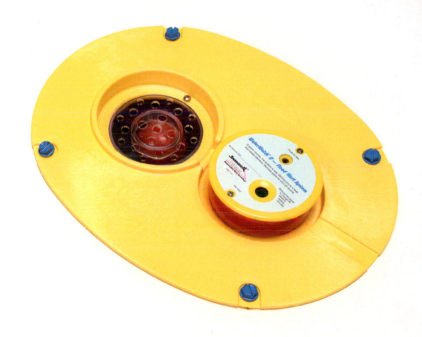

For more info, get my book on crawl spaces, Crawl Space Science.

This is the Reader's Digest version.

CHAPTER TWELVE

PROMISES, PROMISES
Warranties and Service

By now, you probably realize the myriad of options available to you in basement waterproofing. Those options offer various levels of protection against water leaking into your basement. While hiring a contractor who is an authorized Basement Systems dealer will get you what you pay for, one thing is for sure: no matter who you hire, you will never get what you don't pay for.

There are two sides to a transaction. Besides what the seller sells, there is what the buyer buys. Many times the buyer wants to get away with spending less, with overly optimistic hopes of achieving a dry space and then being able to use it. It can work for a time, but one day, in nearly all cases, the buyer discovers that he was wrong in being frugal — to a fault.

Truth in Waterproofing

The reality is: There are no guarantees. A guarantee is saying something won't happen. A professional basement waterproofing contractor cannot say your basement will never flood again. What he or she can warrant is that, if your basement does leak, and it was because of this happening or that happening, then this is what he or she will do for you.

Of course, the warranty depends on what you buy. If water leaks in from an area of your basement that was not specifically addressed, then it is not covered and you will get a proposal for the additional work and expense required to address it.

It is important to understand that a warranty from your basement waterproofing contractor is not a guarantee and not insurance. For example, if you buy a new car, and the car breaks down, you won't be compensated for the fact that you missed your sister's wedding or a day of work because of it. If your basement floods and your stuff gets wet and ruined, your ruined stuff is not covered by your warranty. What is covered is that if additional work is required to get a result that you should have achieved from the work you bought, then it will be provided at no charge.

The waterproofing contractor has no control over what you put in the basement. Some people don't put much there. Others install a beautifully finished room with a home theater system. The stakes are high. This is why all the issues discussed in this book are so very important. There is never any complete guarantee that you won't get flooded again. There are so many variables in a home's construction — soils, water problems, and what people do — that you simply can't say for certain that you will never get flooded again.

However, by choosing the right contractor to do the right things, you can reduce your chance of getting flooded to a statistically insignificant number, and have a great shot at never facing water damage in your below-grade space again. There is little reason why you can't have a reliably dry basement from which to make comfortable finished space.

If you are finishing your basement, check out Total Basement Finishing at www.totalbasementfinishing.com — the best system I've seen — so much so, that we bought the company!

Bluntly Speaking

- Damage to your belongings is not covered.
- Damage to your carpeting or walls is not covered.
- Most homeowners insurance does not cover groundwater leaks and the damage from a groundwater leak.
- Mold growing is not covered by your warranty.
- If you only have part of your basement treated, your warranty is very limited.
- A proper waterproofing system with a SaniDry XP basement air system will inhibit mold growth, but it's not a warranty.
- If you have a single pump system, you will get flooded one day.
- If you have a backup pump system, your chances of getting flooded are tiny, but not zero.
- The floor and walls are two different things with two different warranties.
- There will be some dust from the installation — sometimes not much at all, sometimes a lot. Maybe it will get upstairs, but often you'll just get some in the basement itself.
- The discharge location can be changed at extra cost later if you find you are not happy with where the water is going. This is not a big deal and usually doesn't cost a lot.

Help Yourself

- Don't skimp. Do it right even though it costs more.
- Hire a Basement Systems dealer, since you won't find the solutions in this book anywhere else.
- Report any problems to your contractor right away.

- Annual service is recommended. It doesn't cost much to find a problem before it finds you. When your dealer contacts you to tell you it's time for annual maintenance — schedule it.

CHAPTER THIRTEEN

THE PERFECT BASEMENT

If Money's No Object, Then Do This

Money is an object! Okay, it is. But only if you expected to pay cash for this repair. Most people don't pay cash for an automobile — they finance it. There are all kinds of options to get your basement fixed right: a home equity loan, credit cards, or a home improvement loan, which your dealer can help you with.

If a house is worth owning for what you paid for it, with a wet unusable lower level that causes property damage, frustration, anger and despair, then it is worth owning with a dry usable space for what you paid for it plus the cost to fix it right. Make sense?

The perfect system. A WaterGuard perimeter drainage system with a TripleSafe sump pump system, BrightWall paneling, and a SaniDry Sedona basement air system. Ahhhh!

The Perfect Solution

The price will vary with how big the basement is, the amount of floor area to be covered by carpet, how many windows, which wall paneling system is chosen, etc.

Remember, you are going to spend more than this if you don't fix it!

Now you know the very latest cutting-edge Dry Basement Science. You are an educated consumer and know what to have done to your basement and why. Your local Basement Systems dealer can help you with the items discussed in this book because we know all of this stuff and live it every day. To find your local dealer, call 1.800.640.1500. **Thank you!**

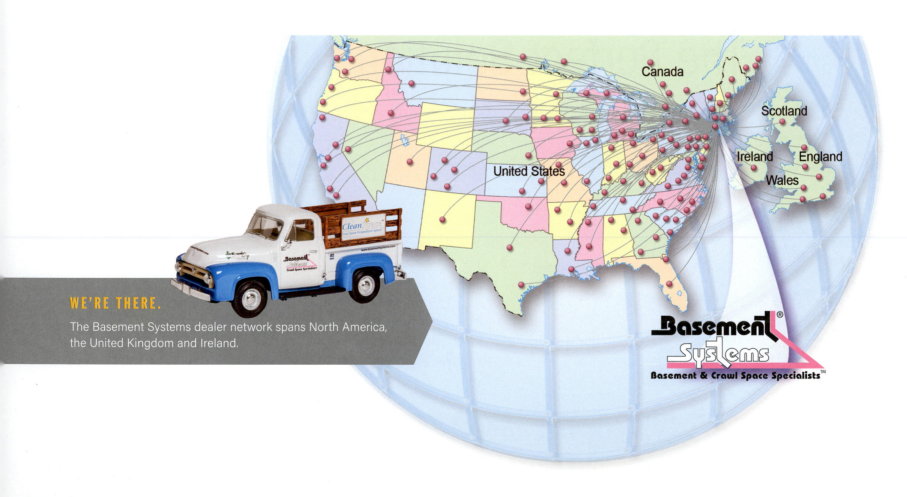

WE'RE THERE.

The Basement Systems dealer network spans North America, the United Kingdom and Ireland.

Looking to Completely Finish Your Basement?

In 2006 a new approach to basement finishing was invented and made available. It's now a sister company to Basement Systems, Inc., called Total Basement Finishing. Your local Basement Systems dealer may be the local Total Basement Finishing dealer, or it may be a separate contractor.

The new system is truly water-, moisture- and mold-resistant. A lot of approaches claim this, but I mean... you can get a foot of water from a big plumbing leak and not have to replace the walls, baseboard, insulation, or flooring! Pump it out, dry it out — no damage! That is a real breakthrough!

If you are going to finish your basement, this is the way to do it. **It will last 100 years without having to be replaced!**

FIND YOUR LOCAL
TOTAL BASEMENT FINISHING DEALER

www.totalbasementfinishing.com | 1.800.640.1500

For more info, get my book on basement finishing, Basement Finishing Science.

About the Author

Larry Janesky is an authority on basement and crawl space repair and building effective businesses that serve homeowners well. In 1982, at age 17, he began five years of self-employment as a carpenter and builder before founding Basement Systems, Inc. Today, Basement Systems is the largest network of waterproofing and crawl space repair contractors in the world. Larry has taken personal responsibility for repairing more than 50,000 basements and crawl spaces over 30 years through his local installation business in Connecticut. Larry is also president of Total Basement Finishing, a leading network of finishing contractors, and Dr. Energy Saver, a network of contractors that provide home comfort services. Larry has trained thousands of talented, dedicated basement repair contractors and their employees in the past 25 years. He holds 30 patents. Larry is the author of Dry Basement Science, Crawl Space Science, Basement Finishing Science, Saving Energy and Money at Home. He has also authored an award-winning novel, The Highest Calling: An Inspirational Novel About Business and Life, Struggle and Success. He writes a daily blog called "Think Daily," received by nearly 40,000 people each morning.

Larry enjoys seeing everyone around him succeed. His mission is to make the world a better place for homeowners, employees, and businesspeople by helping build successful businesses that serve all effectively.

He lives in Connecticut, with his wife and 3 children. He enjoys outdoor activities with his family and is a passionate motocross rider. In 2015, he and his son won the Baja 1000, the longest non-stop cross-country race in the world.

Trusted Partners

Basement Systems Inc. is one of six sister companies with expansive contractor networks. All are industry leaders in their respective fields. Each has developed an informational book like this one about problems homeowners face and their options for solutions. Visit their websites and request a free copy of their books, compliments of our network.

MyCleanSpace.com

BasementSystems.com

AtticSystems.com

TotalBasementFinishing.com

DrEnergySaver.com

FoundationSupportworks.com

Notes